Environments for Outdoor Play

Theresa Casey began her career as a playworker in an adventure playground in Edinburgh supporting the play needs of children of a wide range of ages, abilities and backgrounds but with a particular focus on children with disabilities. Three years in Thailand followed, developing play opportunities for children growing up in difficult circumstances. During that time a playground design developed by Theresa, her colleagues and the children from a Bangkok slum community won an international design award. Since then she has been particularly involved in practitioner-led action research on inclusive play which has resulted in a number of publications and programmes of activity.

Theresa is a Fellow of the Winston Churchill Memorial Trust which allowed her time to study play in Sweden, Finland and the Ukraine. Her work is informed by an international perspective and grounded in the belief that it is the right of every child, no matter their circumstances, to have opportunities for play.

Environments for Outdoor Play

A Practical Guide to Making Space for Children

Theresa Casey

P·CP

Paul Chapman
Publishing

Paul Chapman Publishing
A SAGE Publications Company
1 Oliver's Yard
55 City Road
London EC1Y 1SP

SAGE Publications Inc
2455 Teller Road
Thousand Oaks, California 91320

SAGE Publications India Pvt Ltd
B 1 I 1 Mohan Cooperative Industrial Area
Mathura Road, Post Bag 7
New Delhi 110 044

SAGE Publications Asia-Pacific Pte Ltd
33 Pekin Street #02-01
Far East Square
Singapore 048763

Library of Congress Control Number: 2006936565

A catalogue record for this book is available from the British Library

ISBN-978-1-4129-2936-3
ISBN-978-1-4129-2937-0 (pbk)

Typeset by Pantek Arts Ltd, Maidstone, Kent
Printed in Great Britain by The Cromwell Press, Trowbridge
Printed on paper from sustainable resources

For Jimmy, and Jamie my brown-eyed boy

Contents

Acknowledgements

Much of the inspiration for this book came from the wonderful places for play in which I have been privileged to work, especially Scotland Yard Adventure Centre (The Yard) in Edinburgh and the Foundation for Child Development play projects in Bangkok.

The Play Inclusive (P.inc) Action Research Project, also at The Yard, has given me the opportunity to join in wonderfully questioning and thought-provoking conversations and I am grateful to the talented and committed playworkers there who have welcomed me (and gurgling babies) into their discussions.

Thanks to friends and colleagues who helped me out with Chapter 5: artists Suzie Hunter, Heather Christie and the multi-talented Mark Carr; Robin Sutcliffe, Dave Brady and Patrick Martin of Sutcliffe Play; and Margaret Westwood of many hats. Thanks to Alan Rees for the help with the case study in Chapter 2 and to David Yearley of RoSPA Play Safety and Kate Lander of the Landscape Institute for help with Chapter 8.

I have gained lots of ideas and food for thought by visiting play projects in various countries and keeping my eyes open for how children endlessly reinvent play spaces. It's been amazing to see similar play taking shape from diverse 'ingredients' around the world. So thanks to all those projects and children from whom I have borrowed ideas. The International Play Association (IPA) World Conference in Berlin in 2005 proved a rich source of debate and ideas that also inform this book.

Thanks so much to Emma, Sean, Molly, Eoghan, Jessica, Niamh, Martin and Nicky for the fun play day up in the woods, and thanks *again* to Barbara, Caroline and Veronica Casey and Tricia and Jake Herriot for minding the babies.

Introduction

How do you recognise a great place to play when you see it? Is it the diversity of activity – children running, throwing, chasing, hiding, watching, listening, arguing, shouting, laughing? Is it the world of possibilities – trees to climb, puddles to splash through, swings to soar on, challenges waiting to be tackled, materials to build with, tools to work with?

Is it the atmosphere that says 'whoever I am it is fine for me to be here'? Or conversely, 'we are not supposed to be here but it's too exciting to ignore'? Is it the complex interactions between children and their environment? Or the ability of the space to absorb everything the playing child throws at it?

Environments for play are made up of people and a feeling of place which goes way beyond standard notions of fixed play areas – those swings, slides or multi-activity units in semi-landscaped surroundings. The places where children choose to play are those vibrant, challenging and enticing places that meet their need and desire for fulfilling play opportunities. Beaches, urban streets, back alleys, woods, cemeteries, churchyards, doorsteps, constructions sites and quarries all offer something that children often opt for over what is officially provided for them. These can be enticing play spaces even if (or partly because) they are out of bounds.

From a child's point of view a wonderful place to play can be as small as a doorstep or as wide as the line on the horizon. It can be full of people, familiar or not, or a place to be entirely alone. It can be a hillside with a view of the boats coming in and out of a harbour, or a street corner with a melee of people, sounds and smells drifting or rushing past.

Or, it might be the park, the school playground, a playing field, a garden, a waiting room, a childcare facility – but only if we think very carefully about how that will happen.

We have to see the development of play environments in the context of how children live their lives and make a serious attempt to understand how modern society, with its rules, regulations, cultural imperatives and contemporary paranoias, impacts on their lives – and therefore, on their time and space for play.

We are helped to remember, and to rethink, what an environment for play really is by innovative design in public spaces; by collaborations between playworkers, educators, artists and children, by new takes on old play areas; and by a desire to better understand what children actually want from the spaces in which they spend their time.

Developing environments for play and thereby making space for children is by its nature collaborative. An environment only becomes a play space when it is used by

1

children for play and no amount of compulsion will force a child to enjoy a space that doesn't support that. There are plenty of examples of spaces that offer a predefined, limited set of activities which children will duly engage in for a period of time before exhausting the possibilities – but that is not what we are aiming for here.

We are looking for spaces that expand through children's use of them; that support all sorts of experiences through play; that are enriching, uplifting and satisfying; that offer the possibility of challenge and risk and allow a child to feel secure and confident enough to take these on or not as they choose. Places that are at times messy, awkward, funny, frustrating, breathtaking – and almost always unpredictable.

Ethos

There are three underlying themes in this book:

- *Inclusion.* Article 31 of the *Convention on the Rights of the Child* states that all children have the right to play. We have a clear responsibility in making space for children and to have thought through how those spaces will support that right. How will they support disabled children to play and participate fully? How will they address inequalities amongst that setting's community which impact on children's opportunities to play? How will they foster an inclusive culture in which all children are equally welcome?

- *Children and adults are competent collaborators and partners in the venture.* The views, ideas and experiences of both adults and children are valid. They may bring different and varying depths of experience to different aspects of the development. An atmosphere of listening, responding and respecting each other's experience and point of view should be fostered. Adults have a responsibility to address the imbalance of power between them and children so that it will not impact on children's ability to participate and voice their views.

- *The environment is an important platform for children's play.* While children can and will play almost anywhere they are, the environment has a crucial role in either supporting or detracting from their play. Many children have little choice as to where they spend their time as it is organised into schedules for education, childcare and other activities. Their ability to move freely around neighbourhoods is also diminishing. Therefore, providing space for play has to be seen in terms of meeting children's fundamental needs.

A practical guide

This book aims to be a practical guide, with a range of suggestions from immediately achievable ideas through to long-term development projects, so that no matter what your starting point is you will be able to see progress.

Strategies for education, childcare, integrated services and the development of a childcare workforce all form the backdrop in which practitioners will be working differently and looking for new ways to meet children's needs. Growing concern about the consequences of diminishing opportunities for play is coupled with new requirements on the settings to provide for play. Teams often say that they want to improve opportunities for play with all its attendant benefits but don't know how to go about doing it. Therefore, the intention of this book is to provide you with knowledge, advice, ideas and inspiration to develop play environments that better meet the children's needs and that help you to achieve the outcomes expected of these provisions.

As well as expanding the play opportunities available to children, play environments offer a number of 'side benefits'. One of these is a better and more positive way of dealing with a number of issues with which people concerned with children are grappling; issues as diverse as inclusion, bullying and the need to promote physical activity.

Developing the environment for play and thereby making space for children allows us to replace artificial, adult-led management tools with more empowering, child-centred and playful solutions.

Developing the environment lets us replace:

■ zoning with free-flow, choice and flexibility;

■ taught games with captured lessons;

■ adult management and policing with distant, informed support;

■ age-segregation with mixed-age friendship and play groupings.

The chapters that follow are not necessarily stage-by-stage but interlinked. You will see the benefits of developing the environment for play as soon as you get started. A small change to the environment or talking to the children about it from their point of view for the first time will soon have everyone engaged with the process.

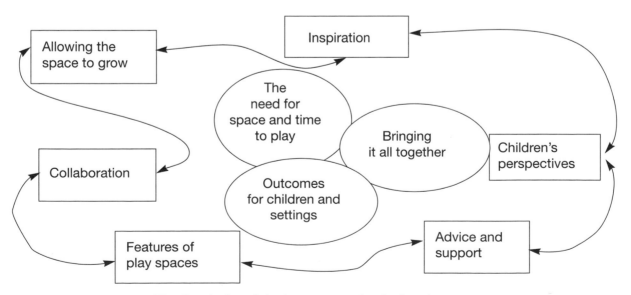

Fig. A An interlinked process to developing play space

Terminology

Children

The reader should assume that when we talk about children in this book we are talking about children with a range of abilities, personalities, needs, backgrounds, talents and interests. And that these can change from day to day, if not minute to minute!

Inclusion underlies all the advice to ensure that the right of disabled or disadvantaged children to play alongside peers, if they choose to do so, is supported. Specific advice or ideas are given if they have been found to be particularly helpful to these groups of children.

There are different views on the use of such terms as 'children with disabilities', 'disabled children' and 'children with additional support needs'. The phrase 'disabled children' is now preferred in some contexts. It reflects the concept that the child is disabled by barriers in society rather than by a particular impairment. There are many children and parents who do not like it, however, since it seems to emphasise 'disabled' over 'children'. The phrase 'children with additional support needs' reflects a broader sense of the requirement to respond to children's varied needs which may change over time. The phrase can encompass a broad spectrum: children who are experiencing difficulties or change, gifted children, refugees and asylum-seeking children for example.

Examples and case studies in this book illustrate types of experience, interventions and processes. Names and details therefore do not identify any particular child.

Parents

Throughout this book I have chosen to use the words 'parent' or 'parents' to mean those people who care for a child: mothers, fathers, foster carers or temporary care-givers, step-parents, grandparents, single parents, heterosexual or same sex couples.

Teams

This book is for people working with children in a wide variety of settings or roles. I have generally used the terms 'practitioners' or 'teams' to include those people who can be involved and contributing. Therefore teams might include teachers, playworkers, play development officers, specialist staff, volunteers, community workers, arts workers, janitors, nursery nurses, learning support staff, parents and visiting staff.

Children's need for time and space to play

Environments for play make up part of the landscape of childhood. Awareness of the local context and wider trends which impact on children's lives help us to develop spaces that better meet their needs.

In this chapter we will look at:

■ Children's need for time and space to play and specifically

    – drawing on one's own resources

    – identity

    – connection to the community

    – social relations

    – contact with nature

    – physical activity.

■ A spectrum of play types.

■ Building up a picture of play opportunities in your area.

There is no doubt that children's access to space and time for play has dramatically altered over the latter part of the twentieth century and the beginning of the twenty-first. Many of the concerns that relate to environments for play are indicative of general global trends – a loss of space, the encroachment of adult management into children's free time, fears about children's use of outdoor space (because of traffic, 'stranger danger', bullying).

Many of these changes give rise to serious concerns regarding the development of children and their immediate and long-term health, wellbeing and happiness. The well-documented increase in childhood obesity and diabetes is noted not only in Hong Kong but also in the UK, in the USA and in Pacific countries. The negative results of inactivity and confinement to indoor spaces will have lifelong implications for those children.

Loss of space for children's play can be seen every time a playing field is sold off for development or when green space is lost to urbanisation. However, it is not just the physical loss of space that impacts on children. Children are excluded from more and more places for play and not just those (such as railway tracks) that are understandably forbidden.

Increasingly rules and regulations bar children from playing in what were once public spaces (shopping centres and malls replace the public space of market squares and piazzas; theme parks replace public parks; school playgrounds fall under the ownership of management companies and are locked out of hours; young people are corralled into skate parks to avoid their public display). Public attitudes often seem to suggest that children's play is a nuisance or even a criminal act and that a child playing outside without adult supervision is neglected, even if they are in the street around their home. These notions are sanctioned through the use of curfews and orders to disperse groups of young people in certain areas and in some countries.

Children's need for time and space to play

The constraints and fears that limit children's opportunities for play, particularly outdoors, deprive children of essential childhood experiences and opportunities – opportunities to develop friendships and negotiate relationships; opportunities to grapple with the full gamut of emotions including those such as jealousy, boredom or anger, as well as happiness and satisfaction; opportunities to take risks, have adventures and misadventures; to have contact with nature and the environment.

It is because play offers unique benefits to children that the right to play is included in Article 31 of the *UN Convention on the Rights of the Child* which recognises:

> the right of the child to rest and leisure, and to engage in play and recreational activities appropriate to the age of the child and to participate freely in cultural life and the arts. (UNICEF, 1989)

Drawing on one's own resources

In our hurried world, time for play as well as space to play can be in short supply for children whose schedules are as full as a chief executive's. Individually, schools, childcare, after school activities and clubs have their own benefits, but do they leave enough time for the child to fall back on their own resources? Are children still having a chance to be bored, to hang about apparently aimlessly with friends, to be unsupervised? Is there time for a toddler to dawdle along picking up sticks? Or for an eight year old to mess about on the way home from school or for an adolescent to set aside their timetable and hang out with friends – or for any of us to take time to assimilate our experiences? If not, then an essential ingredient is missing.

Sometimes making space for children's play has less to do with the physical development of a site and more to do with releasing some time back into children's control – whether that's re-introducing 'recess' or 'playtime' back into the school day, disorganising the programme of a club, or parents taking the decision not to fill a child's week with activity after activity.

It is often adults rather than children who gain most from the planned programme of a club (which can act rather like a security blanket for us). We tend to worry about what would happen should our children become 'out of control' and can be somewhat uncertain as to what we should be doing if we are not occupying the children. And yet, replacing space for children's own agency with adult agendas largely excludes spontaneity, imagination, unpredictability, flexibility – all the qualities we associate with free play.

Creating time for children's play allows them the opportunity to draw upon their own resources. Practitioners can support children's view of themselves as people with a unique mix of skills, talents, capacities and potential. A full life needs us to respond to difficulties we encounter, to face up to conflicts, be flexible problem solvers, to recognise challenges and opportunities when we see them, to learn from difficult as well as pleasurable experiences and deal with disappointment. These experiences in self-directed play provide children with vital opportunities in the development of resilience.

Identity

For children to develop confidence and their own sense of identity it is essential that they go through these processes themselves – these cannot be replaced by adult-managed lessons. Children need opportunities to understand themselves as individuals and in relation to peers and their community. They discover their own preferences, choices and outlook on life, including an ethical outlook. They are striving for independence whilst also struggling with rejection or acceptance of aspects of culture and tradition around them.

> If a child's identity is formed through a complex and fascinating alchemy of environmental adventures and genetic history, then the wider the range of environmental experiences on offer, the more opportunities there are for supporting each child's developmental journey. (Zini, 2006: 29)

Connection to the community

We do not feel a strong sense of connection with the community unless we participate in it – and children's play is one of their most fundamental ways of participating in community life. Children with disabilities are equally entitled. Their right to 'fullest participation in the community' is expressed in Article 23 of the *UN Convention on the Rights of the Child*.

> Article 23 recognizes that disabled children should 'enjoy a full and decent life, in conditions that ensure dignity, promote self-reliance and facilitate the child's active participation in the community'. (UNICEF, 1989)

Outdoor play environments are places where people of different backgrounds and ages can meet. They can provide a focus for community activity and promote social cohesion.

Social relations

We don't really learn how social interaction works unless we ourselves have had the chance to make friends, to fall out, to try and get on with people we aren't immediately drawn to, to sort out disagreements or experience the loss of a friendship. Environments for play have a crucial role in expanding the possibilities for play and therefore supporting children in this.

Within play, rules of conduct, behaviour and interaction come from the children themselves and are negotiated and developed at their own initiative which means that the lessons they learn are particularly deep.

What children learn in schools for example is not confined to the classroom. Captured lessons of the playground can include tolerance, the valuing of difference, and a respect for others, as well as current fads and fashions.

Contact with nature

You could read books about it or watch a video, but a sense of wonder and a connection with the planet we live on are better fostered by lying on the grass to look up at the sky, or by climbing to a hilltop, by skimming a stone on the waves or by letting an insect tickle the back of your hand.

Firsthand encounters foster children's sense of wonder with the natural world

Many children's experience of nature is second-hand and on a scale that can be difficult to grasp. Even those children who do not experience directly the power of the natural world are confronted with media images of disaster and destruction – earthquake, flood, tsunami. We teach them about climate change and how they must now be protected from the sun rather than enjoy it. Children can watch fantastic images of creatures in far away environments, sea creatures in the deepest part of the ocean, snow leopards on a remote mountain side, bats in subterranean caves, and yet they may not know the fascination of watching ants crossing a doorstep or birds feeding outside their window.

The beginnings of a real connection are made at a more immediate and manageable level. Watching children on a beach or in garden we see how they can experience a space and make sense of it using their whole bodies and all their senses. Children benefit from frequently spending time in even a small outdoor space where they can encounter natural cycles, rhythms of life, growth and a rich sensory environment.

The importance of the immediate environment to children is expressed in Hart (1997: 18):

> We should feed children's natural desire to contact nature's diversity with free access to an area of limited size over an extended period of time for it is only by intimately knowing the wonders of nature's complexity in a particular place that one can fully appreciate the immense beauty of the planet as a whole.

Physical activity

The enormous health problems being stored up by children through poor diet and lack of physical activity are waking us up to the damage done to children if they do not have adequate opportunities for outdoor play. This has been shown by research (see for example Mackett, 2004) and it is obvious to most of us watching children at play that they can burn off a lot of calories doing so. Not all children are in to sport and not all of them like organised activities (and those who do probably don't want them all the time), but all children do want to play.

The beauty of play is that it gives children the chance to achieve the necessary levels of physical activity in a way that is motivated by the fun of it, that is different all the time and that develops a pattern of being active that will stay with a child because it is part of their daily life. Play environments can of course restrict or encourage opportunities for active play. 'Keep off the grass' and 'No ball games' rules will be rather de-motivating as will frankly boring areas, while areas with slopes and tunnels, things to jump off and through, exciting things to chase and interesting places to 'hide and seek' will be more energising.

This does not mean that play spaces need to cater for physical activity through stereotypical equipment for running, jumping and climbing. Aiming for a space that supports the wide range of types of play will achieve the same end more successfully through, for example, wild group games of chase or fantasy and imaginative play with flying heroines and fleeing baddies.

A tall order?

So play spaces have to be places where children can dawdle and daydream and also be motivated to shriek and run about! They are places for children to make contact with nature, with peers and with the community; places to take on risks and face challenges but also to maintain a sense of equilibrium. A tall order?

Well, yes and no. Play is by its nature flexible, changeable and multi-faceted so an adequate environment for play is one that provides a platform from which play can take off. It doesn't proscribe certain activities or feelings but does have hints and pathways, suggestions and possibilities.

A spectrum of play types

An issue that frequently emerges in play provision is that some types of play are given a higher value than others. This valuing leads to some types of play being praised and encouraged while others are actively discouraged or even forbidden, as shown in Figure 1.1. Many that are not highly valued by adults have enormous value to children and are understood very differently by children and adults.

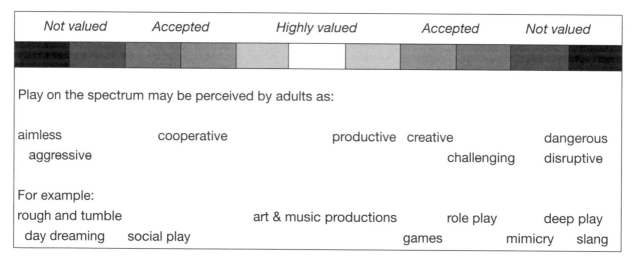

Fig. 1.1 A spectrum of play types and adult perceptions

Source: Based on a model developed in the Play Inclusive (Pinc) Action Research Project by Theresa Casey and Susan McIntyre, 2005

Most highly valued are those types of play that are seen to be productive or potentially productive; play that is artistic, creative, musical, dramatic and that can produce products such as paintings or performances.

Play which demonstrates positive values such as cooperation and negotiation is accepted, but play which is considered disruptive or which causes anxiety in adults is not valued and may be suppressed altogether. This can be play that appears aimless, challenging or aggressive. Playing in the rain, play fighting, play dealing with conflict or difficult issues such as death or gender roles, word play using slang, mimicry and in-jokes may all fall into these categories.

Reflection on perceptions of play behaviour

This activity is based on observation of children at play and reflection on adults' responses to it. It can be based on a 'real time' observation but using a video recording may be more effective. (Ask permission first.)

- Make a video of a session or part of a session. Ask one or two people to watch it through, noting how adults respond to the children's play and particularly which types of play are actively encouraged and discouraged.

- Bear in mind that encouraging or discouraging play can happen in a number of ways including how the space is set out, spoken words, body language, giving someone a 'look', imposing rules and so forth.

- If a video recorder is not available, or if you prefer, allocate one or two people as observers for a session. They can take notes of the types of play encouraged/discouraged and adult responses. They may also like to take photographs as visual prompts.

- Using the notes and/or the video, open a discussion with the team about the responses. Use specific examples from the observation.

- Use a flip chart to list on one side types of play encouraged and on the other those that were discouraged.

- Introduce the spectrum of play types (page 10). How does it compare to your lists?

Questions to stimulate discussion might include:

- Is there a pattern to the responses made by adults?

- Why do we value some types of play over others?

- What concerns us about these and makes us want to halt them?

- What do children gain from each set?

- How can we find out from the children how they feel about different types of play?

- How do the children feel and react when we stop them?

- What could we do to widen the range of play opportunities available to the children?

Involving children in the discussion

You could ask children to act as observers and note takers as a way of feeding their views back into the discussion with adults. They may have an entirely different perspective. Ask them how they feel about adult interventions in their play.

The benefits of play come from children experiencing a wide range of play over time, at a level they choose at that time, rather than only a narrow band approved of by adults.

Perceptions about what constitutes play will influence the type of play space developed. Where there is a perception of play as a very narrow band of behaviours then the play space may aim to cater only for that narrow band. A broad understanding of play and its benefits to children should result in a more all embracing vision.

Building up a picture of play opportunities in your area

This broader picture forms a backdrop to the development of specific, local spaces for play either through one-off developments or within a strategy for play, which should then be put into the context of the children's lives.

Even if you are intending to develop the established outdoor space of an existing setting (a nursery or out of school club for example) and feel you know the children and the community well enough already, it really is important to get some broad understanding of play locally to inform your thinking.

For example, your setting is a nursery in an area in which families feel there is limited outdoor space that is safe for small children to play in. This impacts on the way children play and behave when they come in to your setting. They are only with you for a small number of hours in a week so perhaps also addressing the local play issues will give most support to the children.

This means thinking about the environment for play solidly in the context of children's day-to-day lives (and being sensitive to cultural and gender differences), for example by asking how the experiences available in your service will relate to and perhaps compensate for:

- the effects of local community dynamics;

- the breadth of experiences in the children's everyday play;

- their use of the immediate environment;

- their amount of free-time and how they are expected to use it.

Building a picture of play in the community or area you are concerned with is a vital exercise when considering the development of existing (or the creation of new) play space. It will:

- begin the process of engaging both children and community members;

- help you understand the current use of space and local dynamics;

- help you to identify what is most required and why;

- provide evidence that can be used when seeking wider support and funds for your eventual plan.

It is most likely that a number of methods will be necessary to create a full picture. The number and choice of methods would depend on the scale of the project and local circumstances.

Building a picture of the play in the area – a selection of methods to try out

- Carry out a mapping exercise with the children of their local area to find out where they play, what kind of spaces they do or don't like to play in and why, and what stops children from playing in the places they would like to.

- Bring together children in small groups and physically walk the area together and discuss it as you go. Make sure all the points that are made are noted: a dictaphone is useful to capture the colour of what is said and children can take photos to match up with key points, or draw, write or use symbols to add detail to a map.

- It can be very interesting to find how these places connect and how children travel between them. (Some of the most interesting play 'spaces' are actually journeys between points.)

- Enlarge a map of the area on a photocopier. The children can draw and write directly on it. Again, capturing the discussion on tape or video is always useful as not everything gets written down.

- Give children their own cameras or video recorders to make short photo-documentaries of their area.

- Many children have access to cameras on mobile phones or digital cameras. Use these to download play images to a computer.

- Take a walk around the area and look out for the places children play. Try this at different times of day, different days of the week and, if time allows, at different times of the year.

- Remember that play changes with the seasons and the weather; use that to prompt memories of play experiences. There may also be local traditions, festivals and events that are part of the play calendar.

- Try making a play calendar. On a long strip of paper mark out in sections the months of the year or the seasons. Leave plenty of space in each. Children and adults can mark (writing, drawing or using symbols) the kind of things that they do at different points in the year. Encourage them to put in what they actually do (or for adults what they also did as children) and not just stereotypes such as bonfires in autumn or sledging in winter if that isn't actually the case.

- Any of these can be displayed locally – school, library, community centre, a friendly shop – with simple questionnaires or more maps for people to pick up, complete and return.

▶

■ You could try asking the local newspaper to print a request for memories and memorabilia of play in the area. They might print one of your blank maps and ask readers to return it. Offer a prize as an incentive.

■ Make up a questionnaire and distribute it locally to find out views about play spaces. Tailor it to children or adults but you can ask the same kind of questions. Form the questions carefully though – make sure they are understandable and stick to the main points you are trying to find out about. If possible involve the children in drafting, testing and finalising the questionnaire. Children and community members can also be involved in compiling and reviewing returns.

Some notes on seeking children's views

■ Remember that children will have a range of very different experiences of local spaces. A child who uses a wheelchair, for example, may not currently be able to access all the spaces other children tell you about. A child with a visual impairment might have preferences for different reasons from their peers. Some areas are very territorial so children may feel with these that they are confined within defined boundaries. Children of different ages want different things from a play space in terms of levels of challenge, types of play, support and privacy.

All of these viewpoints, and others, are valid and should be sought to build up a rich picture.

■ The onus is on you to ensure children have a fair chance to contribute their views. You might make an effort to go to particular places to seek children's views – the local special school or unit, a refugee support project, a homeless unit or individual families, for example – and to ensure that the methods you use are appropriate to the needs of the particular children.

■ It would be ill-advised to just go out and speak to groups of children in the community whom you do not know – it may well be misconstrued and you will be unprotected. If you want to do some fieldwork make sure you are backed up by a proper framework, which could include:

– a fully written plan;

– accurate recordkeeping;

– collaboration with local agencies who are known and trusted in the area;

– carrying identification;

– working in pairs or teams and not alone;

– informing local organisations and interested parties (parents, the local police, the community council and school perhaps) about what you intend to do and when.

> - Bear in mind that when children tell you where they like to play this requires trust. They won't tell you about exciting, forbidden places if they think you are going to tell them off, report them, or worse start to invade their space. You will need to establish ground-rules to begin with and inform them that although you will respect what they tell you, if they do tell you something that you think means that they are at risk of harm you will have to do something about it. Make sure you have their permission before videoing or photographing them. You might risk loosing some information or participants but it is better than loosing their trust before you have even started.
>
> (See Further reading at the end of this chapter for more on seeking children's views.)

All of this information gathering will help to create a picture of the local play scene and will be invaluable in identifying the next steps forward. Hold on to all the documentation you have acquired.

What the information gathering might suggest

Not all the issues that arise will necessary point to the development of a new or specific space for play.

- Introducing traffic calming measures or excluding cars from certain areas will be a good way of enabling children to play outside safely if danger from traffic is the main concern.

- Bringing in playworkers to facilitate play in the local streets or park where children are perceived to be 'hanging about' will reduce the likelihood of children being viewed with suspicion or fear.

- If children are worried about bullying or parents are concerned about 'stranger danger', a regular adult presence (community members or paid staff) at a play area will be reassuring.

- Contacting the cleansing or maintenance departments of the local authority or organising a neighbourhood clean-up project may help to make play spaces more accessible if another worry is litter and broken glass. Contacting the local paper about the state of the play space can also be a good tactic if you need to apply some pressure to get things moving.

- Arranging for playworkers to bring interesting play resources on a regular basis to the local fixed play area can help to make it more inclusive of disabled children if they feel excluded.

- Bringing together people with responsibility or interest in developing opportunities for play is one way to find out what resources and support they can offer (see also Chapter 6).

SUMMING UP

There is growing recognition that reliance on fixed equipment playgrounds as we have come to know them does not adequately meet children's play needs and so this is a time when we need to revisit classic ideas (such as adventure playgrounds, urban farms and children's gardens) or look at alternative ways to provide space or environments for play (public space, mobile play provision, street play, for example).

The play that occurs in a specific setting should be seen in the context of children's lives and their general access to opportunities for play. Designing play spaces should take that into account.

For children to really gain all the benefit that they might out of the play environments we create with them, they should reflect and embrace a sense of play as being broad, rich and unpredictable.

Further reading

Alderson, P. and Morow, U. (2004) *Ethics, Social Research and Consulting with Children and Young People*. Ilford: Barnardo's.

Murray, P. (2002) *Disabled Teenagers' Experiences of Access to Inclusive Leisure*. York: Joseph Rowntree Foundation. (Available at: www.jrf.org.uk)

Key stages in developing the play space

Not everyone has the luxury of developing a play space from scratch with the children who will use it. Most of us will begin by working with what we have, to maximise its potential. If you are starting at the beginning and have identified a site or sites, then this chapter will provide a summary of the key stages in the process you will go through. If you are developing a pre-existing space then you have the benefit of a captive audience of children and families to involve!

No matter the starting point, this chapter provides a framework that can be used to get the most out of your space.

The three areas covered in this chapter are:

■ starting with what you've got;

■ key stages in developing the play space;

■ understanding the space available.

An extended case study illustrates points made in this chapter.

Starting with what you've got

Different spaces hold different potential. The obvious starting point is to thoroughly assess what is available, how it matches children's needs and the scale of any plans.

The space available might be:

■ A school playground which could be developed to provide wider play opportunities and a more positive environment as well as being more supportive of curricular activities.

- An expanse of tarmac which needs breaking up into a variety of areas and surfaces.

- A piece of overgrown wasteland which could be made hazard-free without detracting from the sense of adventure and secrecy which children could enjoy there.

- A 'green desert': a large expanse of monotonous grass with no shelter or variation, which requires planting, shelter and focal points.

- A temporary hut or porta-cabin marooned in a boring space which needs to feel like a secure and interesting environment for children.

- A brown-field or gap site with the potential to be transformed into an adventure playground.

- A play area with fixed equipment which needs to provide more stimulating, inclusive and flexible play opportunities for children.

- A series of small spaces in a local community which can be interlinked to allow and encourage children to move from one to another safely, with play experiences happening between them.

And no matter which starting point the same sorts of questions have to be asked:

- What do the children need in terms of play opportunities? How will developing this space fit into the local context and the other play opportunities available?

- Does this space offer the potential to meet these needs? How does it differ from or replicate other play opportunities available to the children?

- What are the pros and cons in going about the development of this particular site?

- Are there technical issues we need help to understand (water table, power lines, access, underground services, ownership)? (See also Chapters 5 and 8.)

In the example below the local primary school playground has been suggested as a site to develop. It may be that after the initial research into play opportunities in the area several sites will be identified, in which case each might be assessed and compared before settling on one or more to progress to development stage.

You may have no choice. The site you must work with is the one you have already! Still, you will want to start exploring these questions to get off on the right track.

INITIAL ASSESSMENT OF THE SITE – A SHORT EXAMPLE

Playworkers in the after school club situated in the local primary school had already researched the local play situation and found that while some of the children had a lot of street play available to them the scope of play is restricted by the physical environment and perceived safety issues. Parents from the refugee population don't feel it is safe to let their children play outside and children with disabilities are frequently absent from the action. It is pointed out that the grounds of the primary school are an underused resource.

What do the children need in terms of play opportunities here?

- More inclusive and varied play opportunities.

- A meeting point where they can get together with other children and feel safe and secure enough to play.

- Outdoor play opportunities.

- For all the children to be able to play alongside their siblings and peers.

Does this space offer the potential to meet these needs?

- Yes, it is close to the children's homes, enclosed and physically accessible.

- There is plenty of space around the school building on all sides, some shelter, some grass and trees, a nice old stone wall to one side and a large expanse of tarmac. It has possibilities but would need some imaginative use of resources and people to realise its potential.

- The children would still have access to street play as well.

Negative points

- To really encourage use of the space playworkers should be on site more of the time which would require significant planning and fundraising.

- A new arrangement may be required for parking cars. Some people will have to be persuaded that the children's need for space to play is as great as their need for parking.

Plus points

- The families coming from the refugee community already have a trusting relationship with the school.

- Developing this space will be of value to all the groups who use the school grounds: the school classes, the nursery and playgroup children, the out of school club and the holiday playscheme.

- The local community will benefit from the school grounds being more child-friendly and providing a focal point for play.

▶

- There is a pool of potential volunteers and supporters to develop and maintain the site.

Other issues

- To access and develop the space in a way which all the partners are happy with will require negotiation with the head teacher and providers of other services.

- An agreement can be drawn up regarding responsibilities for maintaining and caring for the space.

- The local authority can be approached to provide support with technical questions.

Key stages in developing the play space

Having decided that it will be possible to work with this site, Figure 2.1 illustrates the process and the key stages involved. You might refer back to it at different times to remind yourself of where you are in the process or to see whether you have missed something important.

Taking time to understand both the children's play needs and the proposed site is really important and should not be overlooked as it will give you the solid foundation on which to base plans and designs.

It may sound obvious (though it happens surprisingly often) but there is no point in creating a wonderful design on paper that has not taken into account the children who will use it. Similarly a design that works well in one place might not translate to another area, setting or even to another site just down the road.

To help guide you through the overall process each of the key stages shown in Figure 2.1 is explained briefly here.

Understanding the children's needs

As we looked at in Chapter 1, it is vital to understand the play needs of the children who are likely to use the space once it has been developed. Engaging with them early on, as well as giving you access to important information for the design of the space begins a process of relationship-building and sense of ownership over the space that will pay dividends later.

Understanding the space

Having identified a site with potential for development, the next step is to look at it in far greater detail to really understand it thoroughly. Again this will provide catalysts for interesting design and important information to influence plans. This stage provides another set of opportunities to involve the children and community from the start. (You will find more on this throughout this chapter.)

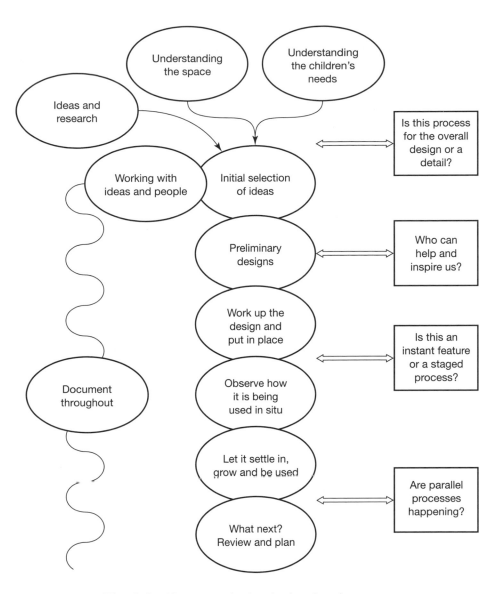

Fig. 2.1 Key stages in developing the play space

Ideas and research

This is a really fun stage when you, the children and any other adults involved can search out inspiring, outlandish, quirky and must-have ideas and bring them back to the design table. One strand should be to look at what has already been discovered by designers, thinkers and practitioners regarding the kinds of elements that make up enriching and inclusive play spaces (see Chapter 3 for more details). The other strand is for you and the children to go and do your own research of spaces and concepts that may enrich your particular site (see Chapter 4 on *Inspiration*, for more details). Trips to other play spaces and to other types of space (such as galleries, gardens, beaches and so on) are enriching experiences in themselves and making it into an investigative research trip gives added purpose. Ideas and research are also sought through talking to people, using libraries and the internet, so there is plenty of scope for involving people in different ways.

Working with ideas and people

Depending on the scale of the project a number of people may become involved and you may wish to seek out those with particular skills and expertise, such as artists, landscape architects, council officers, volunteers and playworkers. Everyone has much to gain through collaborating with people who have different skills and qualities to offer the project. It is important to listen, to learn how to work together effectively and to set parameters that ensure adult agendas and ideas of 'beauty' and 'finished product' do not overtake the goal of creating a space for, and with, children (see Chapter 5).

Initial selection ideas

The previous stages will have brought out a cornucopia of ideas and suggestions – some of them workable, some adaptable, some aspirational, some to file away for another day. You will have thought about both tangible and less tangible qualities that you hope will be part of the play space and about the types of experiences you hope the children will have there. This is the stage for filtering through these ideas and making some selections and decisions that will work in the particular space or spaces identified. (Chapter 6 deals with this process in more detail.)

Preliminary designs

You may want to engage a professional to do this with you depending on the scale and complexity of the project and the skills available in your circle of collaborators – of course you may have a landscape architect, architect, designer, artist or council officer working with you from the start who can undertake this phase. Even if compromises have to be made for financial or practical reasons make sure the design retains the character to which all the preliminary work aspires. (Chapter 6 covers this and the remaining stages in more detail.)

Work up the design and put it in place

Action planning and project management are the key characteristics of this stage – what needs to happen, when, by whom, to what timeframe, at what cost? Will the implementation go ahead in one big push or in stages? Who is going to work on and install the various elements – children, contractors, volunteers, playworkers? Who will oversee the overall process?

Observe how it is being used in situ

As we have already emphasised a space only becomes a place for play when it is being played in. A period of observation and taking stock once the space is being used by children will reveal the successes and failures of the design. It may be immediately obvious that certain features will be used in a way that is different to that anticipated in the design. Other qualities may take longer to emerge. Observation can also include how the design is physically standing up to the way in which children play there and also the quality of experience it supports.

Let it settle in, grow and be used

It may take a while for children to feel comfortable and familiar with a new space and the idea of it being there. Indications of how a space will be used are revealed over a period of time, for example some features only come into their own once the most novel and immediately attractive elements have been thoroughly explored.

In another sense the children's own use of the space can be what allows it to mature and develop. An interest in growing vegetables may lead to the digging of a vegetable plot. Willow is planted to create a cave. Hedges go untrimmed and become wild hiding places. Children bring in loads of planks and tyres to create ramps and bike courses. The planks finally end up as a bonfire and the tyres as temporary seating.

Children's play reveals the value of the environment to them

What next? Review and plan

A play area should never be considered finished – what possibilities would that leave for the children? A period of observation and settling in will have revealed whether the space can live up to the initial expectations. Does it offer the children what was hoped? How are they using it? Who uses it? What gaps have been revealed? Have weaknesses or hazards come to light? Is there scope to revisit any initial ideas that at the time were put on the backburner?

Document throughout

Documenting the whole process has various different purposes which may suggest several ways of gathering and maintaining information and ideas.

As you work through making a wonderful space with the children, you will want to:

- ■ keep track of progress;

- ■ capture ideas and suggestions;

- have a record of all the stages;

- gather material to supply to funders and supporters;

- create a memory bank of moments shared by adults and children (and animals, plants, insects and soil!).

On a practical note, you may find it useful to start a large file divided into sections by each key stage, with each section containing key information, specific tasks, notes, photos, contacts and reminders allowing you to keep track as you work through the process. A simple system for cross-referencing would also be useful, as would a calendar page with reminders of specific events (delivery of a tree, notices to go out for a community meeting and so on) and a weekly or monthly 'To Do' list at the front.

Capturing ideas and suggestions gathered through the range of participatory activities is important as you may come back to these at different stages for inspiration. Creating large scrapbooks is a good idea as they are very accessible and portable and build up an interesting record of the whole process.

Photos taken at various stages are great for 'before and after' comparisons. Do take plenty at the beginning as it can be really motivating to be reminded of just how much progress you have made, especially if energy starts to flag.

Children's own records of the processes they are involved in tie in really well with the various areas of the more formal curriculum.

Most important of all, any documentation showing the community of the setting coming together to develop a space for children really shows how much it is valued. Just as shared memories are planted with the planting of trees and hedges, shared experiences are embedded in the collective memory of the setting's community.

Make a conscious effort to create photo albums and display boards, to send stories to the local paper, create a website or email pictures back to everyone who has contributed.

Understanding the space available

Having identified a site for development, and taken an overview of how to proceed, the next step is to look at the site in far greater detail to really understand it. This will provide:

- important information to influence plans;

- jumping off points for new ideas;

- valuable reference materials for future developments;

- ways of working which involve the children and the community of the setting from the start.

Every site is unique and whether you plan to improve an existing space or have identified a new site for development, you should aim to build up a good sense of the character of that space. This could include:

- seasons and the weather;

- physical features;

- the light;

- culture and history;

- people;

- the setting.

For each of these there are various methods that can be used to gather and record information, with either

- an ongoing approach to gathering information over time;

- or a 'quick picture' approach if the first is not possible or suitable.

You might want to combine the two approaches and ideally involve children in both.

Methods may include direct observation, conversations with children and local adults, research (use of local history, desk-based and internet research) and advice from specialists.

Records and documentation that children help to build up are a really important way of helping them to feel connected to the particular place. The process develops their appreciation and knowledge of the environment from their own first-hand experience and observations.

Seasons and the weather

If you are on an existing site keep a log with the children of how the site is used and any changes that depend on the seasons. Photographic records are good as are children's anecdotes and drawings about what they do and how they play at different times. Keep a note of those parts of the site which become inaccessible at different times of year, perhaps because of lack of shade or shelter or by becoming waterlogged. Accessible areas of planting can become inaccessible if they become overgrown, or conversely, private nooks and crannies provided by greenery may lose their appeal when the branches are bare in winter. Ideally there should be interest all year round with changes balancing off against each other.

Large scrapbooks or long friezes along a wall marked out in months or seasons are great ways to build up this type of record which children will enjoy making and can refer back to.

On an entirely new site it may still be possible to make a year's log before plans really get off the ground – it can take some time. A simple log book marked up weekly will be an invaluable reference later. 'Quick picture' methods will also be useful.

Remember that designing for a typical day at the location and for its proposed usage is more useful than designing for what might be your ideal day. If the majority of days for play at your location are more likely to be overcast, wet or windy, then your design should reflect that rather than focusing on a few precious days of sunshine.

25

'Quick picture'

Without time to record a whole year, try to build up the same kind of picture through conversations with those children who use the site and any adults also (janitor, gardeners, parents, adults who played there in their childhoods). Ask if anyone has old photographs and do a thorough walkthrough assessment of the site (perhaps with a landscape architect or someone from the parks or environment department of the local council).

Again, keep the information presented in an accessible format, perhaps a loose leaf file or document display folder with see-through pockets.

Physical features

Moving around the site with a basic site plan on which to note details and remarks is extremely helpful as it gives a good impression of the site as a whole. A simple drawing would be adequate but try to keep boundaries and proportions reasonably accurate.

Go round and mark up what is there – trees, slopes, water, old walls, boulders, lampposts, sheds, shelters, plants, ponds, old foundations, fountains, basketball or tennis courts, paths, tarmac, dens, caves – whatever you find. This can be done individually, in pairs or in small groups.

Start to think about useable features; what to keep, incorporate or develop and also any hazards that must be removed. Don't be too quick to get rid of anything as quirky features can really add to the character of a site. Sculptures, rocks, architectural forms, old walls, can all help to develop the identity and personality of a site.

This is best done in pairs or small groups and forms the basis for any discussion.

Ongoing records reveal changes in the physical features at different times of year, in different weather or through use by the children. For example, a rainy day may reveal a series of muddy pools and puddles with enormous play potential.

See Chapter 3 for more information on the features of play environments.

Light

Knowing where the light hits the site at different times of the day and year will influence planting schemes and the siting of features such as sandpits, sensory gardens, shiny metal shutes or slides and bird and insect boxes.

Draw a simple site plan marked with the points of the compass and with a separate box for the date, the time of day and the initials of the observer. Photocopy or scan and print a large supply. Make observations on a regular basis and simply sketch areas of light and shade straight on to the plan.

A daily record will be interesting for teams of children to produce by taking turns to make the observations at regular intervals, perhaps every two hours, throughout the day. (Start as early as possible and finish as late as possible to get the best effect.)

Repeat the exercise once a month throughout the year.

Keep these in sequence in a file to give a useable record. Alternatively, stick them together in a long line to make an interesting display which can be folded up concertina-fashion.

The play of light and shadow also has aesthetic qualities that can be exploited. For example architectural forms over flat white surfaces can create interesting formal effects; the shadows from a fence may make stripes on the ground; the sun streaming through leafy trees on to a play space below may create a soft, dappled effect.

Cultural and local history connections

The culture and local history of an area can also be brought into the play space through design in a conscious attempt to maintain or re-establish connections.

As part of an understanding of the space, these aspects can be researched through the local library, local history group, newspaper archives, talking to people and bringing outside people in. The heritage may be urban or rural; work, industry and tradition may be linked to fishing, textiles, agriculture, commerce; community memories may be characterised by change or movement. All of these will have a bearing on the space as it is now.

- Try the library or a local history organisation to gather images of the area. Photograph the same areas now to create 'now and then' pairs of images.

- If you can find some adults who lived in the area as children bring them together to carry out similar exercises as above. They can compare notes with the children and talk about how the area has changed and how their play experiences have differed or have stayed the same.

As well as considering how your setting became what it is now, we can look at it anew with the children to explore their connection with it as a physical and aesthetic experience. Can interest and even beauty be found in small details? How would you describe the walk from home to the play space? How does the familiar stamping ground look from the top of a high building as opposed to the street or vice versa? How is your day-to-day experience coloured by the urban, suburban or rural landscape?

The case study below shows how one project linked its design and development into the history of the local area.

People

All sorts of people make up the community of the setting, some directly and some more indirectly. Find out who is around and might become involved in one way or another. Different events and plans provide different opportunities to involve people.

You might like to start a 'mind map' to generate some ideas on how people are connected and how this might be of use – who can help, who has an immediate connection, who will the space benefit, who will the space impact on, who makes decisions, who would we like to involve, who can donate or lend useful stuff, who has skills to offer?

Every play space should keep an up-to-date contacts file with the names of anyone who can be badgered, cajoled and welcomed into lending, donating and generally supporting it.

27

Setting

The immediate surroundings should also be considered as they may influence the internal design of the play environment. Some factors to take into account might be the proximity of roads and paths, the types of housing nearby, where lampposts are located and natural features. For example, entrances and exits from the site could be placed specifically to avoid tempting children to rush across a busy section of road. It may be better if the entrance is located some distance from pensioner housing or where children waiting to come in may disturb the neighbours.

EXTENDED CASE STUDY: SCOTLAND YARD ADVENTURE CENTRE (THE YARD), EDINBURGH

This case study describes the development of the play environment of an adventure playground over a span of 20 years.

Beginnings

The site close to the city centre had been in recreational use for many years, most strikingly between 1864 and 1889 when the Royal Patent Gymnasium was located there. The gymnasium contained 'ingenious and novel apparatus' such as the 'Great Sea Serpent', an enormous roundabout set in a pond with room for 600 rowers to propel it around, and the giant seesaw named 'Chang' which was 30 metres long and 2 metres wide and said to accommodate 200 people! In establishing the playground a deliberate attempt was made to record the varied history of site and establish some continuity with the past.

The three-quarter acre site was acquired by a voluntary committee in 1986, with a 25 year lease to develop an adventure playground to meet the play needs of disabled children, along with friends, family and the local community.

First developments

This phase was characterised by:

- establishing the basic structures of the site;
- establishing contact with potential user groups through outreach work;
- raising funds and awareness.

The committee took two initial steps. They raised funds and employed a landscape architect to make the first improvements to the site that would make it a useable space. Slopes and hills, a big sandpit, plantings of shrubs and trees, a circuit of pathways and a secure wooden and link fence around the site established the basic structure. The addition of some storage, toilets and a temporary portacabin was enough to allow it to be used by children supported by playworkers.

They employed seasonal playworkers to support creative, play activities on an outreach basis with 'special needs' playschemes in the school holidays. This helped to build links and establish a creative way of working.

▶

First years

This period was characterised by:

- discovering the potential of the site;

- making contacts within the community and with people who could contribute in different ways;

- children, families and groups engaging with the idea of an adventure playground;

- being part-time and relatively small scale.

With small amounts of funds available playworkers continued to be employed on a part-time and seasonal basis. Because the site was still at a basic level of development the playworkers had to make imaginative use of resources to inspire interesting play opportunities for the children – who had a very diverse range of physical, intellectual or sensory impairments, as well as a naturally wide range of play interests.

Group games, themed activities, artistic and creative pursuits were the mainstay of activities. The underdeveloped site was actually ideal for some activities: there was plenty of space to whizz round on the growing range of bikes, trikes and carts; bonfires and barbecues were no problem as there was plenty of unplanted space; the big tarmac area which was earmarked as the site of a building when funds became available was great for playing games of tig.

Energy also went into acquiring resources and contacts to develop the site. An old boat became a fantastic paddling pool in the summer and whisky barrels were planted up with plants and herbs to make landmarks around the site. The Community Service by Offenders' team came in to build raised beds and ramps. The local Episcopalian minister taught the play team fire-eating! Volunteers were involved on a regular basis in play, events and maintenance.

Some big play structures were designed and installed by a local play equipment manufacturer – a fort and slide on a hill, an accessible 'bed swing' and a giant seesaw which were somewhat reminiscent of the Victorian pleasure park. These would last about ten years.

Sculpture projects, woodwork activities, mosaic and murals were all making their mark around the site and the place was feeling more 'bedded in' as a children's place. The playworkers involved the children in designing the first self-built play structure on the site – a tower with hiding and climbing spaces.

In the autumn and winter visits to the centre from groups would tail off as there was little shelter, so the team carried on with outreach work during those times.

The big leap forward

Enough funds were raised to finally build a play centre on site in 1993, so a period of disruption while this took place led to:

▶

- a new phase of outreach work;

- new ways of working;

- a new take on the environment.

As a farewell to the area of tarmac where the building would be situated, a painting day was organised. An enormous frame was painted on the ground and giant painting implements were invented. The children, kitted out head-to-toe in boiler suits, were let loose with vast quantities of donated emulsion paint.

While the building work took place the small team carried on with a programme of outreach activities to school and playschemes. This service was valuable in many ways – it was greatly appreciated by the schools, it developed a relationship with them and helped the play team to have a rounded understanding of their user groups.

By the time the building was opened the playground planting of trees and shrubs was also becoming more mature.

The design of the building complemented the playground well with easy movement between inside and outside – large areas of glass gave a feeling of being close to the weather and the seasons. The open design meant that no activities (apart from bike riding) were designated as outdoors or indoors only and the range of experiences available was multiplied.

The playworkers by this time had less need to concentrate on conjuring up activities but were much more able to set up the site in interesting ways and let the children play in ways they chose. By this time children would arrive knowing what they wanted to do, with plans to take up where they had left off or to find familiar faces or the place they most liked spending time.

Moving forward

- Recognition of the environment as the primary tool of the playworkers.

- More intensive use of the environment as a medium for adventure play.

- New use of the space.

- More involvement by the children in developing the site.

As the playground has developed from its early stages there has been an increased recognition that the environment itself is a primary tool for the playworkers in supporting play. Playworkers spend time on a daily basis setting up the playground with various loose materials and temporary features to stimulate play or to respond to the observed needs of different children. The playground has the feeling of a series of rooms with different characteristics and possibilities for the children, who have a great sense of ownership of the site.

The 'story' playground is documented in words and images and is retold often by visitors and children sharing 'remember when' moments.

SUMMING UP

The children's play needs act as the starting point for all stages of developing an environment for play. Getting to grips with how the proposed site or sites might be developed to meet some of those needs is the next stage, from which the whole design and development process can take off.

Once children are regularly using a space this process does not stop. New children come, the local context and dynamics alter, the space changes and so it goes on, taking on a life of its own.

 Further reading

Clark, A. and Moss, B. (2005) *Spaces to Play: More listening to young children using the Mosaic approach*. London: National Children's Bureau.

Features of enriching, inclusive play spaces **3**

In this chapter we will look at some of the features and qualities that have been found to contribute to successful environments for play.

Included in this chapter are:

■ features of enriching, inclusive environments for play;

■ what kind of experiences will children have?;

■ more on types of play;

■ two principles:

– the importance of allowing play space to evolve;

– cycles of change in play spaces;

■ using longer term, semi-permanent or temporary features (including people);

■ a short case study.

This chapter explores these ideas and offers a number of concrete examples that readers can immediately take away and put into practice.

Features of enriching, inclusive environments for play

The kind of features that support children and their play seem to remain relatively consistent over time. The UNESCO Growing Up in Cities (GUIC) project of the 1990s found that the criteria by which children judged their environments as satisfying their needs had not changed since an original study by Lynch looked at the topic in the 1970s.

> Beyond the provision of basic needs, what the children wanted most was a sense of security, acceptance and positive identity, in places where they could socialise, play with friends and find interesting activities to join or observe. (Chawla, 2001: 21)

Increased interest and attention in the last ten or so years have led to the development of new ways of thinking about places to play and what they can offer children. Playground designers, play practitioners and others in related fields have considered the factors which contribute to successful play spaces. There has been a number of attempts to identify features and elements that will provide children with enriching opportunities for play. The most prominent example in the UK's playwork field is in *Best Play* (NPFA, 2000).

Criteria for an enriched play environment. Play provision should provide opportunities for:

- A varied and interesting physical environment.

- Challenge in relation to the physical environment.

- Playing with natural elements – earth, water, fire.

- Movement – for example running, jumping, rolling, climbing, and balancing.

- Manipulating natural and fabricated materials.

- Stimulation of the five senses.

- Experiencing change in the natural and built environment.

- Social interaction.

- Playing with identity.

- Experiencing a range of emotions. (NPFA, 2000: 35, adapted from Hughes, 1996)

Significantly this provides a broader understanding of a play environment as a place which offers a range of opportunities, rather than being purely a set of physical features.

This was developed further in relation to inclusion, drawing on action research (Casey, 2005) citing five significant characteristics of a play environment which support inclusion. These were:

- flexibility;

- shelter;

- centres of interest;

- natural features;

- atmosphere.

To these were added:

- sensory elements;
- accessibility;
- risk and challenge;
- continuity between indoors and outdoors. (2005: 35)

Bringing inclusive qualities to play environments

Much of the flexibility and variety that support inclusive play can be brought in through natural features such as overgrown shrubs, insect attracting plants, trees, boulders and water. The addition of a variety of loose play resources such as tools, junk, dressing-up clothes and wheels expands the possibilities for play endlessly.

Since all children are unique and their play takes many forms and directions, the wider the variety of play and ways of playing the environment supports the more inclusive it is of children with a wide range of abilities and needs.

Natural features also serve to bring in sensory and aesthetic experiences which, while of particular interest and support to some children (those with visual impairments or children with complex learning disabilities for example), can be appreciated by all.

Layers of sensory experience can be built up with regard to light and shade; colour combinations and contrasts; music and noise as part of the playscape; varied textures in bark, leaves, pebbles and sand; the smell of herbs or cut grass; the sensations of movement through and as part of the play environment.

Breaking the space up and providing more sheltered and intimate spaces can be very helpful to children, some of whom may feel anxious or overwhelmed by busy play spaces. Again, natural dividers and markers such as trees, hedges, slopes and shrubs are really useful. Shelter can be introduced as a permanent feature, such as using a reinstated bike shed, or through temporary arrangements such as a tepee or child-made dens and bases. You will often see children making use of small sheltered spots in amongst shrubs or tucked into corners.

Some children, those with autistic spectrum disorders for example, can be particularly disturbed by sudden loud noises or high pitched sounds whilst others might find the hubbub of a playground difficult to make sense of, so more sheltered areas can be very supportive here.

These attempts to draw together likely features and qualities of successful places enable us to begin to understand the environment we are working towards and working with. They can be used in various combinations to make up survey forms for play areas as suggested in the photocopiable form on page 37, which also includes alternative wording for children.

Child-made shelters support communication and inclusion

What kind of experiences will children have?

This question is really at the root of a successful development process. It goes beyond enquiring about types of equipment or even asking what there will be to do. The idea of offering a space or spaces which supports diverse experiences taps into a deeper understanding of play and suggests that design and development can be play-driven rather than activity-driven.

The range of experiences that children might access could be in the aesthetic, creative, physical, emotional, psychological and social realms. Instead of thinking the children will be able to ride a bike, jump from a climbing frame or paint a picture (activity-driven) we can think about how the space will allow a child to be spontaneous, innovative, flexible or reflective (play-driven).

All play environments will try to offer a wide range of experience but it may be that greater emphasis is placed on one aspect over another. At different times and for different children one well-functioning play space can be:

- a haven of natural green space and tranquility;

- a hub of feverish child-owned democracy, disputes and action;

- a construction site full of never-ending hammering, sawing and building;

- a backdrop to fantastical, imaginary play.

The key to this is really an attitude or an atmosphere as much as design, recognising that if it is a place for play then play is what has to happen, and play isn't a series of specific activities but a messy, unfolding, changeable experiment.

Here are some examples of how to translate this thought into design. The important factor is that spaces have to be allowed to change and intended uses aren't going to stay the same. If the gardening gear all ends up on stage as part of a performance that's fine; if a quiet corner actually morphs into the favourite den in raucous games of hide and seek so be it.

Sample		
Playground survey form		

Location   Date

Note taker(s)

General impression, likes, dislikes, etc.

Tell us what you think! Write, draw, or squiggle in these boxes

Wording for adults   Alternative wording for children

Flexibility	Are there things that you can change and play with in lots of different ways?	
Shelter	Is there any shelter here? What's it like?	
Centres of interest (P.inc, 2004)	Are there any really interesting things to play with? What are these?	
Natural features	Are there any natural things to play with (like trees or long grass or pebbles)?	
Atmosphere	What is the atmosphere like here? Does it feel friendly or not?	
Sensory elements	Are there things ■ To touch? ■ To smell? ■ That make noises to listen to? ■ To taste? ■ That are interesting to look at? Tell us about them …	
Accessibility	Can you get to everything that you want to?	
Risk and challenge	Are there things that are quite exciting and adventurous?	
Practicalities (parking, toilets etc.)	■ Was it easy to get here? ■ Are there nice toilets?	
Any other suggestions, improvements, comments, etc.	Anything else to tell us? Any suggestions for better playgrounds? Write draw or squiggle here …	

A sense of peace and tranquility

- Create a small pond with boulders to sit on surrounded by hushing grasses.

- Use screening such as a willow fence, some shrubs or a dry stone wall to protect quiet places such as a bench or a tree from the general hubbub.

- Build a high lookout point such as at the top of a play structure or a den on a high slope to give a new perspective.

- Create the impression of a courtyard by dividing a space off, loosely enclosing it and siting some central features such as a fountain, a sculpture or a planted bed.

- Take a pile of cushions and some books and set them out on a blanket behind a wind break.

Children's voices

- An outdoor auditorium can be made from logs set out in a horseshoe shape or in concentric circles.

- A temporary stage is simple to build with crates and plywood or wooden pallets.

- 'Meeting spaces' and 'boardrooms' can be available to the children indoors or by dividing outdoor spaces with fences and hedges, building a tree house, erecting a tent or siting a sturdy table outdoors.

- Large blackboards and graffiti boards can be sited on fences, gates and walls.

- A campfire makes a great focal point to sit around and talk.

A construction site

- Build the biggest, deepest sandpit you can manage (a sure-fire winner in any playground).

- Make available real spades, buckets and wheelbarrows.

- Leave at least a few parts of the site undeveloped so that children don't feel constrained about digging or making a mess.

- Provide a solid sheltered area with workbenches, tools and a wood store.

A fantastical backdrop

- Mature planting such as trees and bushes can metamorphose into the landscapes and even the characters in children's fantasies.

■ Basic props can inspire new play scenarios – simple dressing-up clothes, sparkly or filmy pieces of cloth, masks, musical instruments and ropes are all great. Keep them fairly ambiguous – there is much more scope in a selection of interesting fabric than say a fairy or fireman costume which is exactly what it is and no more.

■ Landscaping features such as large boulders, slopes, hollows and hillocks create interesting focal points for the play to roam between.

■ Corners are good – you never know what is around one!

More on types of play

Connected to the range of experience is the concept of play types (which we have looked at briefly in Chapter 1 and specifically in Figure 1.1).

To all intents and purposes you are going to know if the space is working effectively if children are choosing to play there and if the play observed is broad and rich in its scope.

Every so often it is useful to sit back and to carry out a really careful observation to see if there is something lacking or disturbing in the environment which is restricting access to certain types of play. It is helpful to have in the back of your mind a feeling for the wide number of play types that can be differentiated.

The following list of play types brought together by Hughes (2001:15) is helpful in this task:

■ symbolic play

■ rough and tumble play

■ socio-dramatic play

■ social play

■ creative play

■ communication play

■ exploratory play

■ fantasy play

■ imaginative play

■ locomotor play

■ mastery play

■ object play

■ role play

■ deep play

■ dramatic play.

Bear in mind the fluidity of play: when children are playing together all sorts of behaviours, internal processes and types of play can be happening at once.

Objects with which to play, elements to manipulate, people to interact with, time and space to play, and a sense of permission or safety and security are basic ingredients that will allow most play types to happen at a basic level.

Two principles

Two helpful touchstones to bear in mind in the development of play space are:

- the importance of allowing play space to evolve;

- an awareness of cycles of change.

Where does design finish and play take over? To children a degree of unfinished messiness offers more possibilities than a polished design. We are looking for play spaces that invite children to use them and over-designing a space can be as big a problem as careless design.

This is one of the biggest challenges facing us in creating play space. If we see over-designed and under-designed spaces as either end of a sliding rule then there is some place in the centre that offers a good enough range of play possibilities to children, but going too far in either direction will be limiting (see Figure 3.1). The challenge for us is finding the right places on the rule to achieve the best outcomes for particular children in a particular place.

The features and qualities previously described (see pp. 34–5) help to achieve this aim, and observation of the types of play taking place will help us assess how successfully it has been achieved.

Fig. 3.1   A slide rule of design

The importance of allowing play space to evolve

Remembering that a play space evolves through use over time is helpful. The space initially does need to have some allure or invitation for children and it should offer suggestions, pathways and openings to the children playing there. Digging out the biggest sandpit you can manage is usually a good start!

In the early life of a new play space only a basic framework may be in place: divisions of the area into grass, paths and sand; immature planting providing less in the way of hiding places or interesting sensory experiences than it will at a later stage; stark-looking boundary fences or walls; basic play structures in an unembellished state. Children have not yet become familiar with all that the space has to offer or had time to get used to the idea that they are allowed, even positively encouraged, to use it in the ways they choose.

Over time, however, divisions of space will make more sense as the children use them and modify them in different ways; the planting will reveal new ways of playing in and around it; the walls and fences will gain a patina from weather, lichen, art work and graffiti; play structures will be adorned with fabrics, ropes, paint and extensions. A staffed play environment in particular can support major change in the space through staff responding to the interests and prompts of the children.

Cycles of change in play spaces

We are used to thinking about natural cycles as they tend to be seen as an educational learning experience as well as part of developing a personal appreciation of nature and the aesthetics. The season, daily patterns of light and growing cycles sit happily within the formal and informal curricula.

Transformation, creation and destruction are also cycles that have an important place in play spaces and should therefore be accommodated. (Adults tend to have more difficulty with the loss of their own control implied by this.)

In the same way as sandcastles can be lovingly built on a beach only to be lost to the incoming tide or stamped upon with complete abandon, so features of the playground can be created in the knowledge that they will eventually be destroyed or will revert back to an earlier state. Features of the play environment may weather, be lost in undergrowth, decay, or simply be taken apart in the children's search for materials for new purposes – to feed a fire or build an encampment for example. Fragments may be excavated years later in a tangle of shrubs or dug out of the soil.

Using longer term, semi-permanent or temporary features

The features that make up a play environment form a number of layers which have varying life spans, allowing the space to remain flexible, responsive and stimulating. These can be described as longer term, semi-permanent or temporary features, as shown in Figure 3.2.

Thinking about how to make best use of each layer can be helpful for building up the ongoing play potential of the environment. Some suggestions for working with each layer are given below and naturally some suggestions could cross over from one layer to another.

SHORT CASE STUDY: CYCLES OF CREATION, DESTRUCTION AND TRANSFORMATION IN A PLAY ENVIRONMENT

'Piano day'

The old piano in the play hall had finally reached the end of its days. Over the years a tune had been occasionally teased from it, but more often children would bash out angry, crashing noises or use it to make the kind of racket they wouldn't usually allow themselves to make; some children liked to repeatedly press one note with their ear down close to feel the vibrations. It had contended with numerous sticky fingers, spills of juice and splats of paint.

When a replacement piano was donated it was decided that it was time to recycle the old one and get some last play value out of it.

Cameron, a charming twelve year old who had been coming to play since he was a small boy, was now responsible for the next phase of the piano's life. The piano was wheeled outdoors and Cameron took up his stance …

Can you imagine the sheer satisfaction to be found in taking a mallet and smashing a piano to pieces? Cameron swung at that piano and it crashed and groaned until just the metal innards and strings were left standing, surrounded by fractured wood and black and white keys. These and the interesting bits and pieces of pedals and the music-stand were sent off to the art room while the innards were set aside for their next lease of life. They were painted up a little and fixed into place against a fence in a shrubby area to make a new percussive instrument. The children could rattle it with sticks or their hands as they passed by, thrum the strings and feel the vibrations.

Finally, in the bonfire area Cameron piled up all the leftover wood from the piano casing, set it alight and leant on his mallet to watch it burn.

Longer term features

Basic structural components of a play environment (some basic divisions of space, paths, earthworks, hillocks and boundary walls or fences) create the first layer or foundations of the play environment. At this level you can look out for overall form and balance that will allow a natural flow around the space. Beyond this, there are some features of the play environment that you would expect to have a longish lifespan. These features should be chosen and sited very carefully as they will perhaps have to support children's play for all the years they access the space and may be troublesome and expensive to change.

Fixed pieces of play equipment may be on site for 5 to 12 years or so, a tree for 70 years or more, and a large boulder might still be there for great, great grandchildren to sit on!

At this stage you may be thinking about incorporating basic play features such as shelter, water, space to move around freely, natural features or continuity between indoors and outdoors.

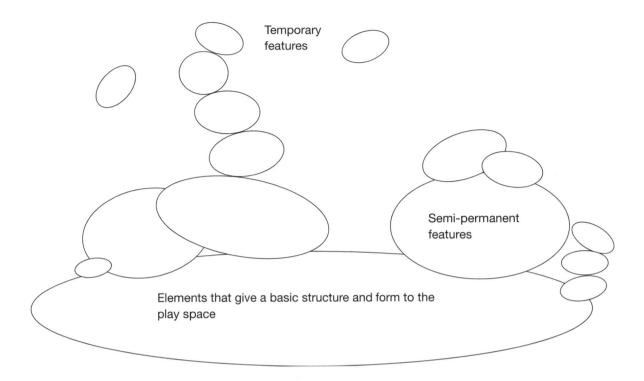

Temporary features

Semi-permanent features

Elements that give a basic structure and form to the play space

Fig. 3.2 Three layers of environmental features

Semi-permanent

Semi-permanent features are those that we would expect to last from one summer up to a few years. They may be introduced to modify the overall space in response to observations of play or direct requests and suggestions from the children. Features such as these could include:

- swings hung between trees;

- an outdoor stage made out of nailed together pallets or an amphitheatre made from concentric circles of logs and barrels;

- transforming a 'wish walk' (a path made across grass or through shrubs by children using it frequently) into a sensory tunnel made out of a series of arches;

- sectioning off an area of the play environment to devote to fires, art, gardening, ballgames, music;

- musical structures – large chimes and xylophones, drums and wobble boards;

- an off-the-ground route around the whole space made up of a series of rope bridges, stepping stones, ramps, seesaws, canyons to leap and walls to scale;

- sheets of coloured Perspex positioned around the space to create new divisions of space, cul-de-sacs and routes with changing light and colour effects.

Temporary

Temporary features may be in place for an hour or a few days or weeks. These elements are an immediate response to what happens in the play space and may arise apparently spontaneously. A supply of art, recycled and junk materials is central to allowing these features to develop. Often by just making materials available a play environment is enough to let play take off in new directions.

- Empty ton bags from builders' yards (edges rolled down) make great mini paddling pools or sandpits.

- A larger paddling pool can be made from old tyres arranged in a circle with a tarpaulin thrown over and then filled up with water. Using tyres and tarpaulins means that it naturally falls into irregular shapes, suggesting 'rock pools', 'bird-baths' or 'hot tubs', and will appeal to a wider age group.

- Plastic tubing and connectors from a plumbing supplier or DIY store are great for making water play systems.

- Playing music outdoors changes the atmosphere – try experimenting with different styles from classical to mouth music.

- Playing with light brings about unexpected new qualities. After dark, put coloured filters over outdoor lighting, project slides on to trees or fabric screens, play by the light of lanterns or simply give children torches to play with. In daytime make 'stained glass' effects on windows and gates with tissue paper or coloured acetate.

- A supply of materials and tools can be made available: straw, newspaper, shredded paper, willow, ropes, logs, string, traffic cones, gas pipes, fabric, plastic sheeting – the list is endless.

SUMMING UP

- There are a number of features, supportive of the breadth of play experiences for children, that can be incorporated into the environment.

- The range of experiences that children might access can be in the aesthetic, creative, physical, emotional, psychological and social realms. We can think about how the space will allow the child to be spontaneous, innovative, flexible or reflective (play-driven).

- Play spaces need to be responsive and adaptable, they need to change and evolve. Bearing in mind the principles of evolution and cycles of change will help.

- Responsiveness, novelty and adaptability can be incorporated as longer-term, semi-permanent and temporary features.

Further reading

Casey, T. (2005) *Inclusive Play: Practical strategies for working with children aged 3–8*. London: Paul Chapman Publishing.

Hughes, B. (2002) *A Playworker's Taxonomy of Play Types* (2nd edn). London: PLAYLINK.

National Playing Fields Association (NPFA) (2000) *Best Play: What play provision should do for children*. London: National Playing Fields Association.

Inspiration

So that new play spaces do not just replicate old ones, it's a good idea to seek out sources of inspiration and put them to use.

If you ask children 'what do you want in the playground' they are most likely to tell you about things with which they are already familiar. Adults especially can be constrained by their own preconceptions of what a play environment or play equipment should be.

This chapter will include:

■ learning from other types of space;

■ research as a source of ideas;

■ field trips and things to look for;

■ expanding the experience.

Learning from other types of space

There are all sorts of places that you and the children can investigate to bring back ideas for the development of your own space. Some you can seek out and visit as a group, others you may investigate through the internet, by borrowing books from a library or by asking someone involved to come and speak to your group and show images.

Inspiring spaces may not be intended for play at all but may be full of 'play value' and have playful qualities that can be translated to use in your space.

Below are a number of suggestions that are worth investigating with just a few ideas of what to look out for. There will be many more possibilities depending on where you live, what is most relevant to you and how far you want to travel. Keep horizons wide!

Spending time on these types of experiences can help to bring a heightened sensibility to the design process (often children are asked for their views and opinions in a much drier way).

Plots and allotments

Market gardens, plots and allotments often have an engaging mix of structure and 'higgledy piggledy-ness'. Structure can be found in the geometrical divisions of space – pathways, raked soil and neat rows of plants at different stages of growth – while the overall structure is enlivened by individual character: flaking paint on sheds, the odd one leaning over precariously, lush sweet peas growing up a wigwam of bamboo canes, yellow marigolds amongst the vegetables to attract pests away, stripy deckchairs set in the shade of fruit-trees.

- Take some inspiration from the combination of orderly division of space and lively features.

- Think about scale – a growing space can be a window box, half of a whisky barrel, a row of pots, a grow-bag full of compost, a raised bed, a square metre field, a vegetable patch or a sensory garden.

- Plant things with different life-spans and qualities – seeds to nurture, bulbs for sudden surprise flowerings months later, pungent herbs for cooking.

- All the accoutrements of gardening are full of play value – watering cans, gardening gloves, trowels, a homemade scarecrow.

A Japanese garden

The 'borrowed landscape' garden and the courtyard garden are distinctive types of Japanese garden. The latter is generally enclosed by the structure of a home, a temple or an inn. The former, in a more open space, incorporates the distant scenery as part of its design – a 'landscape captured alive'. These gardens can also be found outside Japan or may be researched in books and on the internet.

The 'borrowed landscape' garden uses the technique of 'trimming'. This is the device by which you limit what you want to show from the landscape beyond, using walls, thick hedging, an embankment or elevation. These should be unobtrusive rather than eye-catching in themselves, and planting and use of rocks can help them blend in more naturally with the terrain.

The borrowed scenery is linked with the foreground of the garden by means of intermediatory objects (a boulder, seating or sculpture for example). The middle ground scenery functions to bring together the distant scenery and the foreground of the garden into one 'integrated vista' (Itoh, 1988).

- Visiting a Japanese garden can prompt you to think about how your own space relates to and is part of its surroundings.

- Your initial design can make use of the idea of masking and revealing features beyond the perimeter of your space and making connections within it.

- Have a look at the use of unusual and harmonious combinations of materials and the qualities they bring to the space.

Adventure playgrounds

Have you visited a functioning, staffed adventure playground? These sites belong within a tradition of play spaces that is generally recognised as having started in the 'junk playgrounds' of Denmark in the 1930s, and which has developed through different forms and content in the 'adventure play movement' ever since. They include sites which evolved out of children playing in derelict spaces after the urban bombings of the Second World War, construction playgrounds with an emphasis towards children using real tools and materials to build endless rounds of huts, structures and dens, city farms and farm playgrounds (notably in Germany), and the adventure play opportunities for disabled children instigated in the UK by Lady Allan of Hurtwood in the 1960s.

> City farms and adventure playgrounds are joined by a common conviction: that children need contact to nature and develop communicative and social skills best when given space and time to decide for themselves with whom, where and what kind of activity they want to engage in. (Ginsberg, 2006: 10)

The unique qualities of adventure playgrounds go beyond the limited concept of a play space, as suggested by this writer:

> These spaces take on a political aspect because not only do they provide a solution to the lack of supervised and engaging places for children to play, they also represent a defiance of the proscriptive oppression and indifference of the modern built environment. (Claydon, 2003: 29)

- Consider the scope of the children's play within adventure playgrounds and how that is supported by people and resources.

- Living things are crucial to adventure playgrounds and city farms. These can include animal husbandry, small-scale crop production, sensory gardens and environmental activism.

- Bog gardens, living walls (home to insects, birds and plants), ladybird towers, bat boxes, wildflower meadows, hiding spaces for birds, hedgehogs and amphibians (long grass, logs, stones) can all have their place.

The eco-friendly, sustainably-managed project

It may be possible to find a demonstration or craft-based project within travelling distance that can inspire you with ideas for the environmental sustainability of your space.

Fig. 4.1 A habitat for beasties and creepy crawlies

- Grants may be available for developing this aspect of your space.

- Think about generating some of your own power from wind turbines, solar panels, even waterwheels.

- Compost as much of your waste as possible, recycle household packaging into art works and play materials, and think creatively about scrap materials for creating play structures and features.

- Consider how you can collect and direct rainwater.

- Join a scrap store to access a wide range of materials that are often left over from commercial production – rolls of paper, tyres, bubble-wrap and so on.

- Encourage bio-diversity in the space – attract butterflies, insects, small mammals and birds with a good range of native plants.

More suggestions

These are just some of the suggestions you might consider. Here are a few more:

- Urban streets – have a look at shop windows, doorways, street furniture, graffiti, signage, footbridges and underpasses, places people choose to linger, places children choose to play.

Children find adventure in a field visit to the woods

- Beaches, the classic 'loose parts' environment (Nicholson, 1971) – the infinite combinations of water, movement, sky, pebbles, sand, flotsam and jetsam provide endless play possibilities.

- Forests – count the shades of green, climb a tree, hide in the undergrowth.

- Parks and playgrounds – after the initial interest where do the children spend their time and how?

- Art galleries and museums – how is space organised? What makes an interesting display? How are you led from one area to another? What makes for eye-catching signage?

- Garden centres – look out for arbours, sheds, combinations of colour, combinations of sculptural forms and planting, potager gardens.

- Ancient castles and forts – look out for interesting view points high up on walls, peek holes, windows, niches, arrow slots; feel the textures of crumbling stone and lichen; try out scary wooden bridges and precarious spiral staircases.

- Outdoor cultural museums – these may suggest different styles of abode. Houses made from bamboo, mud, palms; homes on stilts, up trees, floating on water, enclosed in forts; a living relationship with animals and nature.

- Local sites of geological interest – quarries, cliffs and caves can reveal the foundations of our landscapes. Look out for use and types of stone, earthworks, and clayworks. Is there a connection with local industry or the character of housing?

- Patterns and structures occurring in nature on as big a scale as Northern Ireland's 'Giant's Causeway' or as small as the honeycomb made by bees can inspire new ideas.

■ Public art – what effect does it have on the space? How are children using it? How does it change the way people behave or interact? What do you know about the artist and his or her ideas? Can you contact them to find out?

■ Environmental art – what does it say about the landscape? Has the artist suggested a different relationship between people and nature? How was the piece made? Can you make use of similar processes? Could you look at your space with an artist's eye?

■ People – talk to older people, folk who have lived in the area all their lives, and newer arrivals and find out about their experiences of space and place.

Fig 4.2 Ancient dwellings translate into play space features

A rocky shoreline offers infinite possibilities and a sense of space and light

Libraries

If you have a well stocked reference library that you can access a trip can be very rewarding in terms of play environment ideas. Useful sections to browse are:

- architecture and landscape architecture (there may even be a small section on playgrounds in one of these);

- art;

- gardening;

- natural history;

- local history;

- geology;

- folklore.

For example a shelf in the folklore and culture categories revealed intriguing titles on stone circles, iron age forts, playground games, earth mysteries, the history of scarecrows, South Sea legends, and fabled cities.

Gardening sections could lead you to Zen gardens, organic gardening, the Eden project, the Arts and Crafts movement, or medieval design.

Other sources

- Delving into family photo albums can spark memories of wonderful play spaces.

- Use the internet – see Chapter 8 for some suggestions.

- Make up montages with pictures from magazines, newspapers, posters and postcards.

Research as a source of ideas

It can be quite tricky to track down sources of information that reflect the whys and wherefores of fashion and thinking in playground design but it is worthwhile delving a little.

Too often projects to develop play spaces are undertaken as if they are without context and with little reference to what has gone before or even to current thinking in the field. It seems that adventure playgrounds have been written about more than other types of play space possibly because they have passionate advocates and they reflect a particular philosophy of working with children. Kindergarten and nursery schools have traditionally emphasised continuity between outdoor and indoor spaces, and outdoor learning environments have had a more prominent place in early years educational practice.

Of late, technical aspects of playground design, meeting rules and regulations and avoiding Health and Safety issues have been more dominant than a pedagogical debate about the role of playgrounds or creativity in design.

While less has been written about development of public play areas and community play developments, there are interesting examples and finding out a bit more will inform approaches to designing new spaces. Aldo van Eyck, for example, was a young architect who was very interested in the ideas of avant-garde art at the start of his career in the late 1940s. The vision he brought to playground design in Amsterdam was influenced by philosophy and art (he was friendly with members of the Cobra group of artists) and used 'elementary, archetypal construction' with a 'powerful simplicity' (Lefaivre, 2002). He used a variety of geometric shapes, small solid shapes that could be arranged in groups and rows, as seats, boundaries or stepping stones.

> The most original and significant aspect of the playgrounds … is the net-like or web-like quality they assume when taken as a whole. They are conceived as a constellation, a scheme made up of situationally arising units – the playgrounds – bound to time, accident and circumstance. (Lefaivre, 2002: 46)

Van Eyck's playgrounds made use of the post-war urban sites and brought them to life as very distinctive play spaces which contributed to the character of the city. They seem to have become part of the landscape of childhood for Amsterdamersin the way that places that children play in frequently can become familiar and part of communal experience and shared memory.

Field trips and things to look out for

A series of field trips planned for children and interested adults is a great way to open up new ideas and to help people to feel involved and part of the process. The difference between a general visit and a field trip is the sense of purpose – you are going to gather information and ideas to bring back to the project. Let it be fun though and of course the best way to find out if somewhere is a good place to play is to play in it.

On a field trip some of the methods you might use to gather information include:

- playing;

- photography or video;

- field trip observation forms;

- observation of play on the site;

- play followed by feedback;

- sketching;

- interviewing and chatting to staff or children who use the site;

- gathering all documentation together into a file or display for future reference;

SHORT CASE STUDY: NEW PERSPECTIVES, NEW OUTLOOKS

A group of children living in a slum community in an Asian capital city were involved in developing a play project in their community. Working with the small play space was a central plank of the team's way of working with the children.

The children's day-to-day living environment was very cramped and little light reached through into the maze of alleyways between the buildings or the small rooms shared by families. The children experienced a lot of change as family members moved in and out of the community. Although they seemed very 'street wise' they rarely ventured beyond the confines of the community and surrounding streets.

The team felt that the children would really benefit from regular visits out and over time made excursions and field trips to a wide range of places offering different experiences.

- A glass lift took them to the highest floor of a skyscraper to look down on the city spread out before them.

- The central city public park was fairly nearby but the children had never been there. They enjoyed the sheltering trees, wide swathes of grass and a lake with turtles and silver-backed fish.

- A bigger group outing was made to a children's discovery park with bikes and tracks to ride around on, and pavilions containing artistic, construction, science and dressing-up areas.

- An aquarium had a cool, blue and ripply underwater ambience.

- The team took children with them when they went to post their letters at the post office further down the street.

- The children experienced different modes of transport using buses, taxis, regular trains and the overhead light railway. This meant going up moving escalators – another new experience.

These visits out and about helped the children to experience the city more widely and to feel they were entitled as young citizens to be part of it. In their visits out the children could experience new ways of looking at things, new perspectives, different senses of scale and movement. They learnt through experience that their immediate environment was not the only possibility. The children took cameras and sketch pads with them when they went out and on returning brought together their images in displays, slide shows and scrapbooks.

Some of what they experienced was directly translated into the space by way of play structures and resources, other experiences were brought back through their play which was expanded as a result, and other aspects were brought back through art works. (Casey et al., 2001)

- a round-up meeting afterwards to identify the most important points and ideas to follow up;

- follow up questions by phone or letter following the visit.

If a group is going on a field trip together then roles such as photographer, observer or interviewer can be allocated to one or two children and/or adults per task.

To give a sense of purpose to the field trip you'll need a list of the kind of things you want to find out to be prepared in advance. These can be picked up through the methods outlined above. Using more than one method also allows you to verify your evidence. For example, if you want to find out which play features on the site are most popular, asking a member of staff, doing an observation and speaking to one of the children might give you three different perspectives.

The following provides a list of some of the things that you might like to think about on a field trip. Not all will be relevant to every visit and you will have your own questions that are important to your specific project.

Basic information

- Name of organisation/site

- Address

- Contact details

- Type of project (for example, adventure playground, city farm, hospital play, forest)

- Aim or special purpose of project (for example, to provide inclusive play opportunities, to offer a therapeutic play environment)

Practicalities (if applicable)

- How is it staffed?

- How is it funded?

- What are the opening hours?

Describe the basic details of the site and location (for example, an enclosed half-acre green space, a small courtyard measuring 20 metres by 40)

Features of the site

- Overall what sort of character does this place have?

- What sort of atmosphere is there?

- What are the main features of the site?

- What are the secondary features?

- In what ways is this site inclusive of children with a range of abilities?

- What are the outstanding features for play?

- What makes it different from other places?

- What range of experiences does it offer?

- Is it a place I would want to play in frequently?

- Are there interesting details or features?

- Is it a good place to play? If so, what makes it a good place to play?

Additional questions for staff and children based at the site

- Is there anything about the site you would like to change or do differently?

- Have you encountered any difficulties? How did you get over them?

- What plans do you have for development in the future?

- Do you have any advice to give based on the experience at your site?

- Do you have any sources of information, advice or support you could suggest?

These are the kind of questions that will help you identify features and characteristics that can be brought back to your project. You might have picked up a general feeling that you would like to replicate, such as 'this really feels like a place for children.' You would then have to think about what exactly gave it that feeling. Or, there may have been one feature that caught everyone's attention such as a water play system or willow maze that you could think about incorporating into your own space.

You are trying to pin down the specifics of what made the space work, so even very open questions such as the one above about the atmosphere can have quite specific answers. For example, if you noticed that sitting at the side of a lake looking out over the water a certain stillness seemed to come over the children, you can reflect on what brought about that feeling – the glassy expanse of blue water, the gentle effect of ripples and reflections, the distant birdsong, the feeling of being small under a wide sky.

■ What quality from this place would you like to achieve? Is it tranquility, privacy, openness, happiness, for instance?

■ What is it that conveys that to you in this space?

Experiencing a range of environments can be an enriching experience in itself from which both adults and children will benefit.

Expanding the experience

You might like to take a less formal and more experiential approach to getting a sense of place (or of course use both approaches). Here are some suggestions:

■ After spending some time using the space in the way you all feel like, ask each person to find an object that would symbolise the space for them. Pick it up, draw it, photograph it or study it closely and try to fix a picture of it in your mind. Gather the group together and ask each person to show the object, or their image of it, that they have chosen and to describe why they chose it.

■ Make up empty frames of various sizes from cardboard. Use these to frame up interesting aspects of the landscape. These can be small details or wide vistas. Framing helps to focus and teaches us to look in a more considered way. In framing you make choices about what to include or exclude and are working with perspective, composition and proportion.

■ Create outdoor 'mood boards'. Draw or lay out a frame on the ground. Fill that frame with found colours and textures that appeal (autumn leaves, stones, pigments in the soil).

■ After spending time in a space, take each other on mini-guided walks pointing out features of the space that you have discovered. These could be allocated in categories such as: 'excitement', 'privacy', 'colour' or 'contrast'; 'twenty-five shades of green'; 'favourite places' or 'inclusive places'; 'how I reached the place I wanted to be' or 'how I got in such a mess'. The idea is to capture some elements of the experience of place that would otherwise be overlooked so the categories can be quite abstract.

■ Jump waves, climb a hill, sit on a fence, hang upside down from a branch, sit in the mud.

Documentation

All the images and documentation generated by these activities should be kept together. It's a good idea to review them soon after as a way of filtering ideas and collecting any other thoughts while they are still fresh in people's minds.

Scrapbooks, folders and displays are all useful ways of keeping information together, safe and accessible.

SUMMING UP

- The play spaces you create can build on ideas and influences you have gathered from all sorts of sources.

- These need not be designated play areas but places full of play possibilities for children.

- Children and adults can both benefit from widening their vision of what makes a great place to play.

- Find the ways that best suit you and the children to capture the essence and features of enjoyable play spaces.

Further reading

Melville, S. (2004) *Places for Play*. London: PlayLink.

Lefaivre, L. and de Roode, I. (eds) (2002) *Aldo van Eyck: The playgrounds and the city*. Rotterdam: NAi Publishers and Stedelijk Museum.

Involvement and collaboration 5

Depending on the scale of the project a number of people may become involved at various stages. Starting with a committee or steering group, you may then wish to seek out people with particular skills and expertise such as artists, craftspeople, landscape architects, architects, joiners, builders, volunteer agencies, playworkers, play equipment manufacturers, council officers and musicians.

This chapter will discuss:

■ what a number of people have to offer and what can be gained through collaborations;

■ working together and setting parameters, including:

   – leaving plenty of play possibilities

   – unintended outcomes

   – risk and benefit pay-offs in play

   – personal safety

   – a distillation of successful collaborations.

Bringing people together is such a rewarding and creative part of developing a space for play. People really are integral to play environments and add to the quirky, unpredictable, characterful personalities that play spaces can take on.

People who have been involved often become part of the network of support upon which the play space can draw.

Committees and steering groups

It's most likely that for a project to be seen through a committee or working group of some sort will have to be set up. In a school, for example, a playground development group may include: the head or deputy head teacher; members of the teaching staff; children representing different year groups; classes or interest groups, a parent representative; and perhaps members of the community with a particular interest.

For an entirely new space starting from scratch it may be necessary to establish a formally constituted group with an elected committee in order to raise funds and meet legal requirements. This chapter will not be focusing on this particular aspect other than to suggest that it is vital that a clear and shared sense of purpose is established early on and that groups should also be clear about the various landmarks that they hope to reach, including how and when they hope to reach them.

To form a group you may need to advertise widely to draw in people with skill, time, experience, imagination and the right attitude. Put notices up locally and make use of the local press. An open meeting can be a useful strategy to find out who is interested. Go out of your way to ensure that meetings are as welcoming and accessible as possible as it will really help as you go along if parents and community members are on board from the beginning.

Artists

Bringing in artists to work on a play space can bring a fresh outlook to the project and help to free up thinking about the potential of the space. They may not have acquired some of the constraints that can seep into the subconscious about what a play space should be, and can be quite tuned in to what feels and looks good. A play environment can be a motivating space for them too as an alternative to gallery environments.

You may ask an artist to work with the overall space, to create objects or play structures within it or to work on a more decorative level. Artists may also be interested in working with ideas about how the whole space is navigated and understood by children (of different ages, abilities and even heights).

Pieces that cross boundaries between sculpture, installation and play structure can be very stimulating to the imagination and help to free up children's play. A fusion of art and play can mean that children are playing amongst beautiful objects and materials chosen for their texture and colour; familiar play objects can be reinvented, such as slides integrated into large-scale sculptures. In their play the children will be experiencing practicality and beauty, function and aesthetics. Art in play spaces can also be used to heighten the sense of discovery and to reveal qualities of the space in a new way.

Word of mouth is often the best way to find an artist to work with and you can also try local art studios, galleries and art agencies. Art students can be great to involve in play projects and can often be recruited simply by putting notices up in a college or student newspaper.

Craftspeople

Having people with craft skills working within a play space is very enriching of a play environment, especially when the results can then be embedded in the design. A metal worker might design sculptures out of broken bikes that then become musical installations on the site. Children see how one object can be transformed into something new and exciting. They can watch the process of working with heat, flames and sparks inherent in metal work. Willow workers can plant young willows on the site with the children, teach them how to tend the willows and then come back to sculpt them into mazes or caves. Similarly woodworkers, paper makers, textile designers and potters can all work on site with children participating in different ways.

Depending on the variables of a particular project, a craftsperson may be brought in to translate a design into a fully realised object or may come in at an earlier stage to help work up a design with the children and help them participate all the way through to making the final piece.

It is useful in that case to break down the stages into bite-sized pieces and to have various ways that children can participate depending on their interest. For example, a textile worker may come in to help with a tent project. An overall design is needed for the shape and structure of the tent; children can design individual decorative panels; the textile worker can teach various techniques to translate those designs on to cloth – dying, stitching, felting. These panels then need to be assembled; a support structure will be built; a tent raising ceremony can be organised; the tent is available for free play, storytelling, games, special events. All of these stages provide numerous ways to involve children.

There may also be a craft workshop or studios locally which would be able to turn designs into objects. Some of these may be very inexpensive options for you, such as employment training workshops or colleges who would take on student projects. In this case it is nice to organise visits to the workshop for the children to see the process that it is taking place. Inviting those people who have made something for you to see it installed is also a good way to establish a strong link.

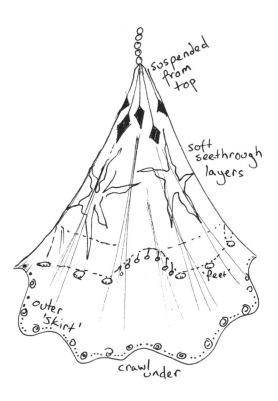

Fig. 5.1 A jointly created tent design

Landscape architects

Landscape architects are specialists in planning, designing and managing external spaces, both urban and rural, and can bring valuable skills and knowledge to a play environment project. As well as technical knowledge that will help in working on the practical issues of the site (user flow, appropriate materials and drainage, for example), they should bring aesthetic and creative aspects to the overall design, be informed about sustainability and environmental concerns, and should be good project managers when necessary.

Like any other professional group you will find some more in tune with your ideas than others, so look at previous projects and areas in which they have special expertise or experience and try to get a feel for their willingness to listen and respond to the needs of your specific project.

Landscape architects (and architects, see below) should be able to translate ideas into scale models or workable drawn-up plans for your group. These can be used:

■ as a basis for consultation with the community and the children;

■ to support applications for funding (and help you to present a professional case);

■ to show the local community what you are planning;

■ to implement your plan and start building!

Architects

A local architect's office can be a good place to seek friendly support. If your play environment plan involves a play building of any sort you may want to talk to an architect about drawing up plans, but they may also be able to help with solving design problems in your space and bring a good eye for detail. Many architects will take on a certain amount of work for voluntary organisations or local groups at a reduced rate or with no charge, or they may be able to help you access funds for the development of plans through architectural associations. Tell them about your project and enthuse them with why it is worth supporting!

Joiners, carpenters and builders

If you intend to embark on a self-build project for any part of your play space (a play structure, wooden bridge, walkways, or forts and dens for example) then bringing in the skills of a carpenter, joiner or builder will help you produce something that will stand solidly and withstand weather and general wear and tear for longer.

If, for example, you and the children have drawn up plans for a wooden tree house you can ask someone with the correct technical skills to check these over first, make suggestions, source the materials you require and teach you and the children the techniques required to actually build it. You could ask someone to work with you and your group throughout the build or to come and check it over at key stages to ensure it is being built safely and correctly.

If you have brought a group of volunteers or parents together with your team to work on the build, it gives them a chance to learn new skills and put these to use – and will probably result in a much more satisfactory product at the end.

Fig. 5.2 First sketch for a tree house

Volunteer agencies

For one-off tasks team volunteering can be a great way to get the job done. Going through the local volunteer centre if you have one nearby is probably the easiest way to organise this. You need to identify a specific task from your plan that could be completed by a team from a local organisation who would also use it as a team building exercise. The task needs to be achievable within a specified time-span (one or two days perhaps), using general rather than specialised skills. The types of task suitable might be digging out a wildlife pond, building a simple wooden structure or decorating a hut as a play team base for example.

You should provide clear details of the job you require to be completed, refreshments, expenses and information about your project. You would either provide materials yourself or could agree that sourcing the materials through donations or fundraising would be part of their challenge. It would also be necessary to discuss beforehand whether children would be on site at the time, whether they would be involved in any way and any codes of conduct (regarding smoking, appropriate language and behaviour around children).

Other teams willing to take on specific projects include those from youth projects (the Prince's Trust in the UK for example) and also groups of offenders undertaking supervised work for the benefit of the community. Contact a local Probation or Community Service by Offenders department to find out more.

Playworkers

Almost without exception play environments will be enhanced by suitably skilled, experienced and, ideally, qualified playworkers who bring a specific skills set to facilitating and supporting children's play processes. (Employing playworkers may well be an integral part of your overall plan.) If your group does not as yet include experienced playworkers then talking to some who have worked on the kind of site you are interested in developing will be invaluable. If you have made a field trip to a staffed space that you and the children really enjoyed then you could invite the playworkers back to make suggestions and share their experience.

Playworkers are also increasingly employed as 'play rangers' working in parks and community spaces and their knowledge of the local play scene and of developing play opportunities will be useful to you. Establishing inclusive play opportunities is another area in which playworkers can enhance the experience children have on site both through facilitating and supporting the play itself and by working with the environment to ensure it is varied, flexible, stimulating and welcoming.

Traditionally, working with the physical environment in order to support and expand children's play was seen as central to a playworker's role, particularly within the adventure playground movement. However, increasingly playworkers are employed in settings with limited access to the outdoors and so have fewer opportunities to develop their skills in relation to it. Therefore you would benefit from seeking out schemes that emphasise outdoor play, environmental play, natural play, adventure play and so on, in order to access this particular expertise.

Play equipment manufacturers

Throughout we have been emphasising process, collaboration and organic growth of a play space, but this doesn't mean that pieces of bought-in play equipment definitely won't have a place in your play space. You may choose not to have any at all or discover as you go along that there is simply no need, but you may decide that one or more pieces of manufactured play equipment would suit the space you are working on.

The key here is to see them as elements within the overall design and to think about how they would enhance the whole space and the experiences available within it, rather than making a shopping list from catalogues at an early stage. (Indeed simply putting the catalogues away until you have done the groundwork would be a good tip.)

Before approaching a manufacturer make sure you have a good brief referring to the kind of things that you would like to happen in the play environment and then see if there is equipment that will help that to happen. Make sure you are creating the right playground for the client group and the neighbourhood. If you are quite certain you just need a basic item such as a swing, then you could simply shop around for the cheapest deal on offer. For anything more complex or subtle you should look for a manufacturer who is interested in ideas about play and inclusive design, and who is willing to be flexible and to spend some time discussing your needs. Don't be afraid to go to more than one contractor or manufacturer for different pieces.

Council officers

Many local authorities now have a designated person with responsibility for play. Finding out who that person is may be the toughest challenge, since play covers many areas of responsibility including recreation, culture, housing, education, health, public spaces and parks. Playgrounds and play development may also rest within different areas of responsibility. Do start with a phone call to your local authority or council to find the person you need to speak to.

Play development officers or units may be able to:

- give general advice and support;

- support consultation and design processes;

- support or join a committee or steering group;

- help you access funds;

- advise you on specific areas such as risk management or inclusion;

- lend resources;

- help you find your way through red tape;

- point you in the direction of people with expertise and experience;

- help you tap into existing networks with an interesting play space;

- advise you on the authority's position regarding particular areas or sites;

- help you in your choice, purchase and installation of equipment.

Sound artists and musicians

Sound artists and musicians may be part of the repertoire of people you bring into the play space to widen and enrich the opportunities that children have within it. They can be a good source of advice about bringing out the potential for sound as a play element within your play space.

Remember sound does not have to be music and sound experiences do not have to come from musical instruments.

Sculptures that incorporate sound can intrigue and tweak the curiosity of children especially if they have to figure out how to get a noise out of them (creaking levers, knobs and peddles, handles to wind, cogs and wheels to turn).

It is possible to buy in outdoor musical and sound features such as large-scale chimes, glockenspiels and drums, but you can have a go at making your own by using recycled materials or commissioning a sound artist to make site-specific installations.

Siting is really important to make the most of these so that children are able to experience them relatively uninterrupted, but also in order that they aren't continually intrusive or a cause of complaints from the neighbours (in the case of loud drums for example, or even a triangle which can cut through everything else). Siting amongst trees or shrubs can be really effective. The space around the instruments should accommodate children sitting together, with enough room for larger groups to come together with handheld instruments brought with them or for instruments to become part of other forms of play (role play, fantasy play).

Sound can become part of the playscape through locating elements around the site to be discovered and experienced in different ways – chimes hanging from trees, rough surfaces or railings to rattle sticks along, water trickling across different surfaces, tin cans on strings, wobble boards, echo chambers, bells. They can be a stop-off point where children can linger or make a racket in passing.

Asking around and using the internet are probably the best ways to find a musician, sculptor or group who specialises in making sound and music for outdoor spaces.

Fig. 5.3 Sound as part of the playscape

Specialist organisations (see also Chapter 8)

Don't overlook those organisations that have been working in play spaces and advising on their development for a long time! Some have particular specialities: Learning through Landscapes, for example, advises in the UK on the development of school grounds. Many countries also now have national bodies promoting the child's right to play which can provide a variety of support which may include all or some of the following:

- access to resource libraries;

- support from development workers;

- databases of play consultants, designers and other play-related professionals and organisations;

- access to research;

- examples of good practice;

- evidence to support your case for the need for play space for children;

- advice on legislation;

- help in finding relevant local government and council support;

- suggestions for sources of funds.

Working together and setting parameters

Working together with people who can bring in fresh ideas and skills can really help to enliven play spaces and provide the children with new realms of play. Working with children may be new to some of the people you involve and that also allows them an opportunity to see things differently or work in more innovative ways.

It is important to set these contributions into a framework so that the ultimate goal of creating a great place for children to play is achieved. Setting parameters may initially include discussion of some of the following:

- rather than aiming for a finished product, create a design and features that leave plenty of possibilities for play;

- unintended outcomes – realising that children will use the play environment in many different ways, some of which will not have been thought of or intended;

- risk and benefit pay-offs in play;

- personal safety.

Leaving plenty of play possibilities

Adults have a tendency to look for a finished product, but as we know a play space for children shouldn't reach an entirely finished state otherwise the world of possibilities in change, transformation and creativity is diminished for children. Professional training might have taught adults to aim for a beautiful, harmonious, polished or, in particular, a 'fully realised' outcome. And yet, you will be asking them to create not just objects but possibilities for how they can be used; not a complete design but a framework that the children can then take in their own directions.

That can be very challenging for many trained professionals. An architect for example might have a vision for a scheme that makes a particular statement and may have thought it through right down to the colour of the skirting boards, whereas what you actually wanted was a blank sheet as a backdrop to children's play.

Similarly, artists or craftspeople working alongside children do need to let go of their own aesthetic enough to be open as to how the children will experience it. They need to be able to tune in to different senses of scale, pace and notions of completeness that different children will have.

Designing either the whole space or elements within it essentially holds a stumbling block. A group of volunteers might think it is a great idea to turn the simple play structure you wanted into a pirate ship with all the associated paraphernalia, but while it might look good at the outset it is imposing their idea on the future play of the children who will use it. Fairly abstract designs with lots of different possible uses tend to be far more successful in the long run.

Paying attention to detail is important however – beautiful solid wood may be appropriate for one design while rough old bits of plank will be perfect somewhere else. Taking the time to countersink individual screwheads matters when children come to play. Being careful about heights, widths and gradients contributes to inclusive play as does thinking about the whole sensory environment.

Unintended outcomes

Some of the people with whom you collaborate may not have worked in a play space before, so it is up to you to ensure that they have a sense of the open-ended nature of play and that children will use the play environment and features within it in ways they choose – which may not be those that were first imagined or intended.

Features need to be sturdy enough to withstand robust play or sited and signalled in such a way that affords a degree of protection from inquisitive users. If a feature of the playground is obviously inviting the children to use it in a way that the adults did not really intend then there is little point in fighting for the original use. You may however have to make some adaptions to ensure that it is not hazardous or easily broken by the way children are using it. For example, if children are using a sculpture as a seat for hanging out and chatting there's nothing to be gained in telling them they are only allowed to look at it and appreciate its aesthetic qualities, but you might need to strengthen it so it doesn't collapse under them.

Risk and benefit pay-offs in play

The person with the overall responsibility for the play space will need to keep an eye on levels of risk and challenge being built in. They should be able to explain to other people the benefits of a degree of risk to children, but also must ensure that anything introduced does not pose an unacceptable hazard to children at play.

As a general guide 'hazard' could be described as those dangers which are hidden or beyond the capacity of children to assess for themselves. Acceptable risk does not necessarily wipe out the possibility of accidents, but it is visible to the children as something that they should make choices about and whether and how they tackle it. Unacceptable risk poses a danger of serious and permanent injury or death.

Risk is not a fixed entity as children's ability to assess and negotiate it for themselves varies. Variables in the play environment itself can cause fluctuating levels of risk – think about the effect of different weather conditions, combinations of children of different ages or abilities, how busy or quiet the play space happens to be. Assessing risk is therefore an ongoing task and adults in a play environment need to monitor it on a low key but continual basis as they work with the children.

Although it can feel as if there is pressure to ensure the children do not come to any harm at all, we have to accept that accidents and injuries do happen. It is not necessarily a failing of the practice or environment if a child hurts themselves. On the contrary, it is difficult to make the concept of a safe play environment stand up. If we try to eliminate risk altogether than we are removing the excitement and challenge of play and diminishing the experience for children. The result would be a de-motivating space for children who would no doubt seek out challenge elsewhere, often in spaces where the risk of serious harm is more real – amongst traffic on busy roads, near railway lines or on building sites for example.

By ensuring that the possibility of risk is retained in the play space, we are providing children with the opportunity to:

- learn to recognise and assess risk for themselves;

- test and expand their own capacities;

- experience the emotions associated with negotiating risk – anticipation, satisfaction, confidence, exhilaration.

Personal safety

Once again the person with overall responsibility for the play environment will have to assess the degree of supervision required for different people coming into the space. Often it is supportive to have a playworker anyway who knows the children working alongside, say, a crafts worker or volunteer. You should make explicit to anyone who comes to help in any capacity the setting's own child protection policy and guidelines and what is expected in terms of behaviour from adults.

Children derive satisfaction from negotiating a degree of risk

Similarly, it will depend on circumstances and the legal requirements where you are whether or not a criminal record check is required for people who come in to help. Often it will depend on the length and nature of involvement, and their potential contact with children.

You also have responsibility to ensure that there are safe working conditions compatible with Health and Safety legislation, that you have suitable insurance arrangements in place and that you have budgeted for the cost of materials and volunteers' expenses.

A *distillation of successful collaborations*

- ■ Be open to working in different ways.

- ■ Encourage an atmosphere of working together and respecting a whole range of skills and expertise.

- ■ Set clear parameters.

- ■ Give plenty of time for the process.

- ■ Finds lots of different, bite-sized ways for the children to be involved.

- ■ Make sure people have an appropriate space to work in and all the materials and tools required.

■ Embed products into the environment.

■ Say thank you and keep in touch.

SUMMING UP

■ The potential for creating an intriguing and motivating space for children's play can be expanded through collaboration between people who bring a range of skills, experience and outlooks.

■ Fresh thinking, creative approaches and new ways to solve design problems are amongst the benefits to be gained.

■ Successful collaboration will be supported by starting with a shared understanding of the special requirements of a play space, such as the need for versatility, flexibility and open-ended design.

Further reading

Children in Scotland (2006) *Making Space: Award winning designs for children*. Edinburgh: Children in Scotland.

Bringing it all together

Chapter 2 introduced us to the overall process illustrated in Figure 2.1. Further chapters have worked through the stages of initial research and ideas gathering which involved:

- understanding children's needs;

- understanding the space;

- ideas and research;

- working with people.

This chapter goes on to lay out the process for bringing all of this together to create an achievable design and plan of action:

- initial selection of ideas;

- preliminary designs;

- work up the design and put it in place;

- short case study;

- observe how it is used and let the design settle in, grow and be used;

- what next? Review and plan.

The underlying principle that all children should be enabled to participate through choice in a way and at a level they choose continues throughout this process. Some children will seek out artistic involvement, others will enjoy the formal design process, whilst still others may prefer an organising role. In this chapter there are again many opportunities to support children's participation.

Initial selection of ideas

The previous stages will have brought out an abundance of ideas and suggestions, some of them workable, some adaptable, some aspirational, some to file away for another day. You will have thought about both tangible and less tangible qualities that you hope will be part of the play space and about the types of experiences you hope the children will have there. All of this will have resulted in a rich stream of documentation.

This is the stage for filtering through these ideas and making some selections and decisions that will work in the particular space or spaces identified – and you will need some methods for doing this.

You will also need to think again about the question of where design finishes and the play and players take over.

You may decide that this task of filtering and reviewing ideas is one for a small group or alternatively an opportunity to share what has been found out with the wider community of the setting or locality.

It is important that you remember to point out to people, especially in a wider consultation, that the preferences indicated will be used as a guide and not as hard and fast decisions, since ultimately a number of factors will have to be taken into account such as:

- finances and resources available;

- compatibility with the location;

- making the right play environment for the users;

- the development of a coherent design;

- a realistic and sustainable plan.

One or more of the following approaches to reviewing the research documentation should be suitable for your project.

Display visually

- Display all the documentation right round the walls of a room, on display boards or across a table.

- Put all relevant research images and notes on to a computer and display. These could be shared electronically or even set up as a temporary website to allow distant access.

- Make up the documentation into a large scrapbook and if funds allow make a small quantity of copies.

Present orally

- Give spoken presentations of particular themes, qualities or ideas (see below) backed up by slides or PowerPoint images.

- One person can be designated to summarise information from different sources or a number of presenters (children and adults) could present their own findings from field trips or research.

- Set up a poster presentation. Groups of ideas and suggestions from field trips and research are set out rather like display stalls, with one or two people who can talk about them stationed at each. Others can go from stall to stall to hear about and discuss the ideas.

Make groups of ideas

Ideas gleaned through research can be grouped together according to:

- themes, for example water features, wild spaces, havens, adventures;

- type/scale of space, for example ideas for very small nooks and crannies, for awkward spaces such as steep slopes or corners, or for wide flat expanses;

- inclusive qualities, for example interesting use of sensory features;

- less tangible qualities, for example tranquility, purposefulness, motivating, energising

Fig. 6.1 Some things to do with fences

Find out how people respond

Depending on how many people are involved at this stage the following methods might be useful:

- A quick way to assess preferences is to give people a set of sticky dots and ask them to stick them onto displays or scrapbooks to indicate their preferred ideas. These can be complied to give a quick reference as a guide.

- Give each person a list, on individual sheets, of what has been displayed and ask them to tick preferences and add comments. These can be compiled, again as a guide. This could also be done in pairs which would be useful for anyone with literacy, learning or visual difficulties.

- Use video or audio recording to capture people's views.

- In small groups simply ask people to feedback verbally and take notes.

- Leave the large scrapbooks with groups such as the local youth club or support base, or in the reception area of your provision, so that feedback can be gathered using the previous methods.

Filtering out less favourable options and highlighting attractive ones

You might find it useful to develop some broad guidelines that would allow you to filter out some options early on, as the following example shows.

Broad guidelines for initial filtering in and out of ideas, developed by the children and staff of the Hewitt After School Club

Filter out:

- anything that is too fashionable or faddy as that will date very quickly;

- anything that seems to encourage gender stereotyping in play;

- anything that that would emphasise rival football team allegiances.

Flag up with a star-rating:

- ideas that reflect what we know about children – that they are thoughtful, active, creative, interesting individuals;

- ideas that seem particularly compatible with our site and the surroundings or that reflect our local history;

- ideas that will be used by children of different ages and abilities;

- ideas that children will be excited about and pleased to keep coming to over a long period of time.

Other points that might help when filtering ideas in and out include:

- remembering the lifespan that different elements potentially have;

- looking out for conflicting suggestions which wouldn't be compatible for the particular site (for example, one enormous play structure that rules out the possibility of a series of smaller, more flexible spaces);

- not being too quick to get rid of ideas that you are not sure how to use – it may be possible to adapt them or retain the essence of them through imaginative design.

Preliminary designs

At this stage you need to be bringing the whole concept together. You have a wish list of the kinds of experiences that you hope children will have on the site, lots of imaginative ideas to help you achieve that, an understanding of the site and ideas about how to make the most of it all year round, and you are bearing in mind that the initial design will be a platform for play which will develop and evolve over time. You know that you will have some long-term features that need to be put in place but that other features are going to be semi-permanent or entirely transient.

So, time to get it down on paper! You will know by now whether there is someone in your group of collaborators who has the skills and confidence to actually draw up the plan. It can certainly be a work in progress and go through a number of sketches before you achieve what seems to be the balanced design you are looking for.

Don't be afraid to get a large sheet of paper with the outline of the site and any fixed features drawn on (to scale) and simply draw and write on to it until it starts to come together, as in Figure 6.2. You might also have drawings or photos, again to scale, of any features you are keen to get on site early on. Cut them out and move them around the larger piece of paper until you find the right place for them.

If you have a lot of overdrawing on one piece of paper, simply draw over the lines and features you have settled on with a heavy, dark pen and then trace it for a neater final version, as shown in Figure 6.3. You can also find computer design packages which you or the children might find useful.

Either way, when pulling the design together bear in mind:

- flow around the site – how will children move from one area to another?

- relationships between areas – is there some logic to the division of space and does it provide for cross-over between areas of play activity? Have any conflicts inadvertently been created?

- are 'pockets' being developed within the overall space that have their own characteristics and are semi self-contained?

- the preference for simplicity and abstract qualities in the overall design;

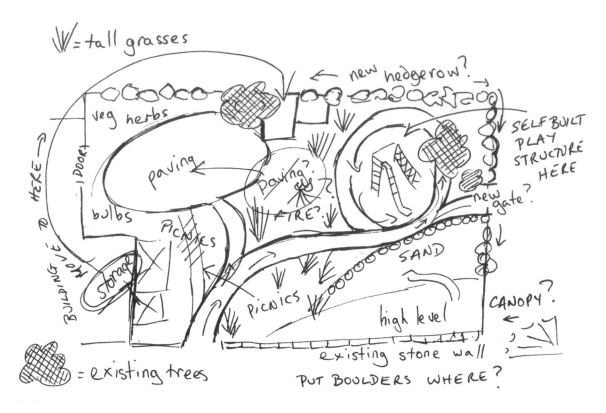

Fig. 6.2 A preliminary design as a work in progress

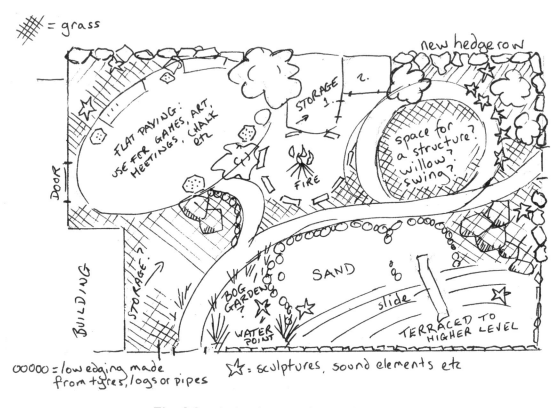

Fig. 6.3 A sketch towards a settled design

- potential for change – is the design flexible enough to cater for additions and adaptations over time?

- scale – are variations in scale making best use of the outdoor space?

- setting – does the design relate comfortably to its surroundings?

- accessibility – are there a number of ways to navigate the space and access various areas? Are the entrances and exits suitable, particularly for families and people using wheelchairs?

It could be that your own drawn version is all you need to move on to the next stage of implementing the plan, particularly if there is little in the way of major work that needs to be completed.

You may however decide that this is a good time to involve an artist, landscape architect or architect, if you haven't already done so, to translate these designs into workable plans. This can be particularly useful if you will be working with a number of contractors for elements such as large earthworks, the installation of drainage or lighting, the varying levels of terrain, and the building of boundary walls or fences.

For a large or complex design someone like a landscape architect may be contracted as a project manager or you may find that it is possible to manage this within your own team.

You may also need to check over the design, or features within it, to ensure that they comply with regulations. A local authority play development officer or a national play organisation should be able to help or point you in the right direction. (See also Chapters 5 and 8.)

Work up the design and put it in place

Action planning and project management are the characteristics of this stage:

- what needs to happen?

- when should it happen?

- who is responsible?

- to what timeframe?

- at what cost?

The implementation of the plan may go ahead in one big push or you may decide that a staged approach is more appropriate. A staged approach is particularly useful if no alternative space is available for the children to use in the meantime.

Simple planning tools will be useful to make sure that the steps are carried out in a logical order and all the preliminary work has taken place. For example, if the main planting schedule is for springtime when do you need to prepare the ground? If you plan a community build for some tree houses before the start of the long summer holiday have you planned a timetable for acquiring materials, recruiting volunteers and training them in basic techniques and Health and Safety? Are you quite sure that heavy equipment such as diggers won't be rolling across the site the day after you have planted up a large grassy area?

Each task can be broken down into preliminary arrangements to be made (ordering materials for example), tasks on site (building or installing for example), and follow up arrangements (maintenance checks for example).

It is inevitable that plans will go astray from time to time but building a schedule really carefully will help. A large, simple, week-by-week wall chart can be perfectly adequate or you can find computer-based scheduling tools.

If compromises have to be made for financial or practical reasons it is important to make sure the design retains the character that all the preliminary work aspires to. A staged approach would be one way to do this by breaking down the site plan into sections and tackling it section by section as resources become available.

Also bear in mind that elements of the overall design can be tackled in different ways. For some parts of it you may be better off bringing in a specialist rather than economising, whereas there may be parts of the plan which can be achieved by working with a team of volunteers. Some elements can be built by children and staff or parents together.

Check carefully that each stage, element or installation is completed to an appropriate standard and bring contractors or builders back if you are not happy with the standard of work.

SHORT CASE STUDY: A SAND PIT PLAN THAT WENT AWRY

We planned a wonderful new sandpit for the children and enlisted the help of some young army recruits to dig out the area for us. We'd thought out the design carefully to incorporate it into the surrounding space (as illustrated in Figure 6.4). There was to be a low bridge right across it that would allow direct wheelchair access from one side to the other and at the same time would add an interesting dimension to the space, dividing it into two areas and allowing children or adults to sit on the edge dangling their feet over the sides. A series of large and small boulders were placed over to one side both as a feature of the sand area and as a link to the play spaces behind.

Spades, buckets and sieves were at the ready. The boulders were in place, the sandpit was almost dug out and the sand was due to arrive, but the rain arrived first. In torrents. Before we knew it the sandpit was simply a huge, muddy pool.

Of course what happened in the ensuing days when the rain kept topping up the pit resulted in the best, most hilarious, most memorable play days the children could have wished for – leaping off boulders into murky depths, lying belly down in the sticky sludge, soaked through already and sitting right down into buckets of water.

Once the sun finally dried up the reservoir and the children had helped to fill it with sand, bucket-by-bucket passed along a line, it was hard for the new sandpit to compete with the memory of the muddy pool.

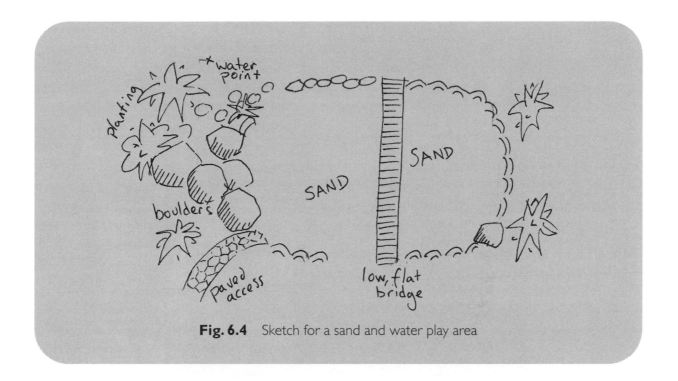

Fig. 6.4 Sketch for a sand and water play area

Observe how it is used and let the design settle in, grow and be used

The way a space is used by children will change as they become more familiar with it and test out the possibilities. Children are quick to cotton on to how adults expect play equipment to be used and then to set about ruthlessly subverting this. Spending time in the play space and paying attention to how it is actually used after it has been established are always worthwhile.

It may be obvious which elements are not likely to be successful or are not robust enough to withstand lots of attention. Alternatively, aspects you expected to be pretty low key might emerge as real favourites.

Ideally you should make a point of carrying out observations in the play space at fairly regular intervals over a period of time, say every six months or a year, to really get a feel for its success or otherwise. In a staffed site this will happen naturally in the course of the day's work, as nursery teachers, playworkers, playground supervisors or head teachers spend time with the children.

You will be looking out for indicators such as:

■ types and variety of play occurring;

■ 'hotspots' of activity;

■ flashpoints in areas which suggest conflicting activity (an obvious route between features crossing an arty space for example);

■ neglected areas or features;

Children will always find their own way to make the most of a play environment

- whether there are ways for all the children to become involved;

- indications of the children modifying the site themselves through their use of it;

- signs of damage and excessive wear and tear.

As well as observations, feedback should be sought from the children about those features of the space which they enjoy, what they would change, how changes to the environment have changed how they play and who they play with.

It can take time for gaps to be revealed in the types of play the design supports, so it is worthwhile giving it a chance to settle in. Planting in particular can take a number of years to mature enough to start to bring about the desired effect. The whole atmosphere and character of a site can really emerge when trees and shrubs have started to gain enough height and density to create hideaways, tunnels and secret places, or to mask fences or unsightly neighbouring views.

A new feature may take a battering initially either through sheer popularity or as a target for vandalism, but if it can survive an initial few months it is likely to have a long life! It can be worth persevering in patching up something that repeatedly seems to be coming to grief. Certainly, get rid of any visible signs of vandalism as quickly as possible so that a disheartening air of neglect does not overtake the site.

Try to stay relaxed about the children modifying the site themselves as this shows that they are really engaging with it.

What next? Review and plan

A play area should never be considered finished – what possibilities would that leave for the children? A period of observation and settling in will have revealed whether the space can live up to the initial expectations.

- ■ Does it offer the children what was hoped for?

- ■ How are they using it? What gaps are revealed?

- ■ Have weakness or hazards come to light?

- ■ Is there scope to revisit any initial ideas that had previously been put on the back-burner?

A new cycle of consulting, planning and design can then take place to modify the existing design or add to it. Again, think about the best ways to involve children in filling any gaps.

SUMMING UP

- ■ Careful decisions should be made in reviewing the source material and filtering it. The selection of ideas can include some for immediate implementation and others to return to later.

- ■ It is important not to let the space become over designed but to leave plenty of scope for the children to develop it further through their own play. At the same time it should be enticing enough to draw children in.

- ■ In order to working up the design and deal with project planning you may like to bring in a professional, but for many projects it is perfectly possible to do this yourself. There are many sources of help and advice to draw on.

- ■ The proof of the pudding is in the eating. Time is needed to allow the children to play and the space to adapt before the successes and weaknesses of the design are revealed.

- ■ New cycles of design and development can begin.

📖 *Further reading*

Hendricks, B. (2001) *Designing for Play (Design and the Built Environment).* London: Ashgate.

7

Outcomes for children and settings

The process of creating a great environment for outdoor play must make a difference to children, expanding their play opportunities and the scope of their play. Children benefit from improvements to the available play space but there are also considerable benefits beyond individual children which encompass the staff teams and the wider community of the setting.

This chapter will look at:

■ changing the way we manage play spaces;

■ access to play environments in children's services;

■ outdoor play environments supporting children's rights;

■ a sense of place.

Changing the way we manage play spaces

Adults are often the arbiters of children's use of the available environment. When it comes to it, it is usually adults who establish the 'terms and conditions' for play – making the rules, allocating time for access to the outdoors and generally setting the tone for play behaviour.

Making changes to the environment also implies working with children in a different way. We are trying to expand possibilities for children but in order to do that we have to be open to them ourselves.

The best way to develop a greater understanding of play is actually to spend time with children at play, being alert to the subtleties and nuances of the interactions taking place. Spending time with children in a range of different environments highlights the impact the surroundings have on the children's expression of play. While some aspects of the environment serve to restrict the scope of children's play, others through qualities such as scale, variation, novelty or challenge, serve to energise it.

The process we have worked through has given plenty of opportunities to do both these things and has highlighted playful values such as choice, spontaneity, freedom, meaning-making and ownership. Having arrived at an environment that fosters this broad vision of play, the way the space is managed should then reflect it.

We will now go on to look at four aspects of play environment management that tend to be fairly common, especially when the playground or behaviour within it is perceived to be a problem. Alternative approaches are suggested to zoning, taught games, adult management and segregation by age. That is not to say that these approaches might not have some value, but that they become less necessary when the play environment is functioning effectively.

Replacing zoning with free-flow, choice and flexibility

Zoning is seen most often in school playgrounds as a way of providing for different types of activity and often to stop football dominating the whole space. Typically zones will include a place for football or other popular ball games, quiet, creative or environment areas, and equipment-based play areas. While there is value in ensuring that a wider range of activity can take place and also in dividing the space up into smaller units, this approach does not take into account the fluidity of play. It puts certain types of activity into boxes so that they are not in conflict with each other. Playing outside the 'box' becomes the problem that has to be regulated.

An alternative to this is to think about the kind of atmosphere and opportunities that everyone would prefer in the playground (such as friendliness, support and caring for each other and the environment) and then to address those. This would suggest modifications such as providing sheltered and comfortable spaces to interact and escape the hubbub, encouraging bird and insect life, planting native plants to tend and supplying interesting nooks and crannies and new focal points so that is possible to play with different children. All of these can reoccur within the overall space and provide links and destinations which will encourage flow around the whole space.

Adults who are engaged with play are more able to provide friendly support when it is needed because they have become more familiar and more sensitive to play. Children themselves are a great source of support to each other when the tone of the playground is set as a place where children's different ways of playing are encouraged and respected.

Replacing taught games with captured lessons

Reintroducing 'traditional games' (such as skipping, hopscotch or peevers, and rhyming and clapping games) is a popular strategy for introducing positive play experiences particularly in schools, holiday play schemes, after school provision and so on. Often older children are taught these games and then become games leaders or tutors to younger children. Many children really enjoy these sessions and they provide positive opportunities for children to interact with each other and engage in active play.

A warning signal might start to flash when they are brought in because, in the view of some adults, the 'children don't know how to play any more' or 'have no imagination'.

The great chroniclers of children's play culture, the Opies, observed back in 1969 that 'the belief that traditional games are dying out is itself traditional; it was received opinion even when those who now regret the passing of games were themselves vigorously playing them' (Opie and Opie, 1969: 14). The belief that children 'don't play like they used to' is still widely repeated and similar views have been found to be prevalent around the world (Bishop and Curtis, 2001).

Our own observation of children at play is likely to show us that play is as vibrant, quirky and lively as ever, but perhaps not expressed through the same games and language as we once used.

It is often the case that the effects of a poor play environment are blamed on the children. In a very monotonous space, for example, children have to rely on themselves to liven it up and might resort to a lot of rough and tumble play, or become aggressive or destructive out of sheer frustration. This can lead to the assumption that the children have the problem.

Taught games should not be the only strategy for supporting play, as the aim is limited (generally to providing more 'positive' play and physical activity) and does not include the goal of supporting children's own creativity, inventiveness, culture and expression through play. It also gives the older children a task (albeit a voluntary one) to occupy their time rather than addressing their play needs.

Our approach to supporting play through the environment should start with a respect for children's contemporary culture of play and for their capacity to meditate their own relationships and interactions. Plenty of abstract, loose materials act like props and give children greater means of expression. Often the play that emerges deals with themes that are important to the children, whether from their own lives or from the media, giving them a way to explore them and respond. Through this freer play children are establishing amongst themselves shared values and codes of behaviour.

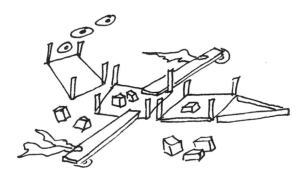

Fig. 7.1 A sketch of a 'plane crash' scene created by children within play from 'loose parts'

Replacing adult management and policing with distant, informed support

The more adults impose a structure on play the more they cast themselves in the role of regulators and managers of what happens. This is neither the most comfortable nor enjoyable of roles. Children quickly pick up on the idea that the adults are there to receive their complaints and sort out problems for them, thereby reinforcing the idea to everyone that doing away with the role would mean a descent into chaos.

Showing a greater interest and appreciation of children's play helps to turn this role around and provides more positive opportunities for supporting play. Children are on the whole able to resolve most issues amongst themselves and even if this causes some difficulty at the time, it puts the onus back on them to work through to a resolution. By doing so they are using and gaining important social skills which they would not be able to do if an adult stepped in too soon each time.

When adults have spent time developing more rapport with the children and tuning in to their play, it becomes easier to empathise within the play situation and to recognise where support could most usefully be given. Commonly there are children on the margins of play who find it difficult to engage with others. Sensitive adult support can help to include these children, in a number of ways that do not overtly highlight any particular child.

Again, the environment itself is a useful tool. Possibilities might include:

- building on their interests in a way that is attractive to other children (such as creating an outdoor art corner full of interesting materials, building a makeshift course for roller skating – whatever their interests would suggest);

- creating an interesting focal point for play (such as a den or a campfire) that children will naturally be drawn towards and so provides a different way of interacting;

- drawing the child in to imaginative role play by helping them find a role, possibly teamed up with you to start with until they are confident enough to take off on their own – this means the adult really getting into the spirit of the game, running around chasing monsters for example.

For some children communication is a barrier and it can be difficult to keep up with the cut and thrust of verbal communication or the subtleties of body language during play, in which case the adult may act as a support to that communication, helping the child to remain involved. Sometimes that will be through interpreting what is happening in language they can understand, simplifying or picking out key points amongst everything that is being said. It could also mean using your own body language, to reinforce excitement, surprise or anticipation, to help the child recognise what the others are expecting and prompt them onto the next stage.

By making improvements to the environment the adult is already providing more opportunities for children's autonomous play and those changes are also supporting broader, more inclusive aspects of play. There will always be children who need support at least some of the time and the backdrop of an improved environment means that adults can provide this more effective but less obtrusive support.

Replacing segregation by age with mixed-age friendship and play groupings

Generally the reason give for segregating children's play areas by age is 'safety', protecting smaller or frailer children from the more robust play of older children. This seems more necessary when large areas of a play space are dominated by one type of physical play, a pattern encouraged by hard-surfaced areas with little variation. In play environments in which the space is broken up, is more varied, has softer landscaping and which caters for a broader spectrum of play, this sort of segregation really starts to seem unnecessary.

Children benefit from the opportunity to play in groupings of older and younger children in the same way that siblings might.

- Games are passed from one group to another.

- Play skills are picked up and developed.

- Social interactions have more dimensions such as caring for younger children, trying to emulate the bigger ones.

- Play is modulated differently to accommodate the different abilities of children.

- Friendships need not be confined to children of the same age.

Within the play environment it is people to play with which creates much of the energy and drive for play, and so variety in players is as stimulating a factor as variety in physical features.

Access to play environments in children's services

Concerns about children's safety outdoors coupled with a broadening net of services for children (and parents) are factors that lead to children spending increasing amounts of time within adult managed settings and consequently diminishing amounts of time out and about under their own agency. These services can include:

- longer hours of 'wraparound' childcare;

- care for older age groups;

- after school activity clubs;

- homework clubs;

- the trend towards delivering a range of services under one roof (particularly in schools).

In some cases these will result in children spending large parts of the day in very similar surroundings and much of it without access to adequate outdoor play opportunities. In England and Wales, for example, the extended school concept includes in its 'core offer' childcare from 8am to 6pm all year round.

When children are not involved in formal education the settings they spend time in should support their need to do their own thing, in their own way, alone or in the company of others as they choose. They need to be seen as diverse individuals whose time is actually their own. They want some privacy and autonomy, but also at times support and encouragement. They need space to move around freely, to make a lot of noise and to use their whole body expansively. They need a space that is meaningful to them, that supports their identity and sense of connection. They need opportunities to do what children are driven to do – that is to play.

It is highly questionable whether services for children that do not offer access to excellent outdoor environments can be considered suitable for them. It could also be argued that providing good outdoor play environments does not completely compensate for the loss of the ability to roam in widening circles of the neighbourhood, to access a range of permitted and forbidden areas and utilise them through play.

We can say with confidence however that children's experience of a provision, whether specifically intended for play or not, will be significantly enhanced through regular access to a high quality play environment. In those settings which are used by children for significant amounts of what is essentially their free time, there is a positive duty for adults to ensure that they have access to outdoor environments for play which will support their own spontaneous play behaviour and activity.

Not to do so, places a heavy restraint on the in-built drive that leads children to play.

Experience of children's services is enhanced significantly through access to outdoor play

When asked about what would improve their lives children consistently ask for more places to go and things to do. Scotland's Commissioner for Children and Young People found this in 2006, for example, when she surveyed children regarding the priorities for her office (available at: www.sccyp.org.uk). A UK-wide survey for the UK national play day (2006) found that 80 per cent of children would rather play outdoors than in. This comment from an eleven year old reflects her concern about children spending extended periods of time in childcare provision.

> My cousins, who are four and six, go three times a week. This is OK, but eight 'till six five times a week is unacceptable for children. Everyone needs some time at home to relax and see their family. It should be illegal, especially for three-year-olds! (Available at: wwwteachernet.gov.uk/ wholeschool/extendedschools/kellyhotseat/)

Those with responsibility for children's services (at all levels) should ensure that:

- play is given a prominent place in strategic planning;

- outdoor spaces for play are treated as an essential ingredient for good quality services;

- staff teams have access to playwork training, professional development and qualifications.

Developing outdoor environments for play can become a shared project for services that come under one umbrella or share outside space.

Networks of projects and organisations with an interest in play can support inclusive play at a broader community level by mapping services for children with additional support needs, identifying gaps in provision, working out which children have adequate access to play opportunities (informal or through play services) and those children who are excluded or overlooked. Networking events can provide an opportunity for the sharing of information, experience and resources.

Outdoor play environments supporting children's rights

We have already mentioned Article 23 and Article 31 of the *UN Convention on the Rights of the Child* (1989): disabled children's right to fullest participation in the community, and the right to rest, leisure and play respectively.

Article 24 recognises the right of the child to the highest possible attainment of physical health. Regular access to outdoor space not only pushes up levels of physical activity, but promotes mental and emotional wellbeing and equilibrium.

A good outdoor play environment can go some way towards compensating for the loss of children's play opportunities and makes a vital contribution to their growth, wellbeing and happiness.

For some children the outdoor environment, in a setting including workers skilled in facilitating play, may be one of the few chances they have to thoroughly immerse themselves in satisfying play. These may be children going through periods of stress or upheaval; children with disabilities or additional support needs; children who are vulnerable because of difficulties at home, economic or immigration status; homeless children;

children from different ethnic, religious and cultural backgrounds. For these children, regular play opportunities in a supportive environment can make a huge difference to their lives.

Opportunities for play are vital to children's sense of belonging as suggested by the following observation which links play to inclusion in schools, but could equally apply to other children's settings.

> From the children's point of view, experiences at play are crucial to their experience of inclusion since they are central to the child's peer relations, self-esteem, sense of identity and sense of connection with the school as an institution or community. (Casey, 2004: 3)

Play environments are also great places for children to practise the skills which will help them form and express their own views and opinions. Articles 12 and 13, respectively, recognise the child's right to express their views freely on matters that affect them and the right to freedom of expression. A play environment can help children to become confident communicators using a range of means of expression (art, music, dramatic play, the spoken and written word).

Play provision should encourage children to listen to and respect other people's points of view and to develop empathy with other people's needs and standpoints. Within free play children are constructing individual and shared identity and an outlook on life which will inform the views they will hold.

All of this means it is not difficult to make links back to political agendas. While we would not say that we are setting aims or goals within the individual child's play (that is, imposing a predetermined outcome on their play), we can say that good enough environments and good enough support create the right conditions for children to gain the wide ranging benefits of play.

A sense of place

Places that children choose to play in are imbued with meaning. Their interests, concerns, fascinations and fears permeate the space and give that elusive 'sense of place'.

For all that adults can do in creating a play environment, they can do no more than offer a backdrop for play and hope that in it children will find reasons to linger.

We can (and should) use knowledge, experience and insight but we cannot provide a definitive best place for play since the combinations of people, environment, culture and context are infinite – which is the beauty and fascination of the whole enterprise.

It is often said that the difference between space and place is the meaning and sense of connection that are attached to the latter. Children's primary and natural mode of meaning-making is through play. They explore and strive to understand their world and develop a sense of their place within it.

We can foster children's natural curiosity with ready access to natural places and direct contact with life forms and the elements. We can offer informed companionship and examples of care towards the environment and each other. We can appreciate the forms that children's play takes (and them as individuals) and share in the awkwardness and the joyfulness of play.

Ultimately, we need to remember that children are happier when they have places to play.

SUMMING UP

■ Making changes to the environment also suggests that we should think about how we work with children and whether that needs to change too, in order to really open up the possibilities for satisfying play experiences.

■ Regular access to a high quality play environment will significantly enhance children's experience of a provision, and there is a positive duty by adults to ensure that they have access to outdoor play.

■ Outdoor play environments support children's rights, in particular Articles 12, 13, 23, 24 and 31 of the *UN Convention on the Rights of the Child* (1989).

■ Children with enriching, satisfying, challenging and readily available places for play are happier children than they would be without them.

Further reading

Lester, S. and Maudsley, M. (2006) *Play, Naturally: A review of children's natural play*. London: Children's Play Council (available at www.playday.org.uk).

Troubleshooting and sources of advice

8

In this chapter you will find sources of information and advice:

- national and international play organisations;

- a selection of interesting and inspiring websites;

- other play specific organisations and contact points;

- play safety and standards;

- useful contacts – rights;

- the environment and environmental issues;

- landscape architecture;

- advice on funding.

Nowadays a great deal of information that will be useful is available on the internet including up-to-date regulations, academic and position papers, visual examples and advice.

Postal addresses and phone numbers are provided here for some key organisations, but on the whole websites are given as a starting point.

The following contacts offer a range of help including fact sheets, telephone advice, resources and databases of play professionals/organisations. Contact individual organisations to find out what they can offer.

Every care has been taken to ensure that the information given is up-to-date and accurate, but do check out sources of information for yourself to be sure you are confident with it. A wide range of contacts has been provided but inevitably the list is not comprehensive. National and regional organisations for play should be able to provide you with more details.

National and international play organisations

The Children's Play Council
8 Wakley Street
London
EC1V 7QE
Tel: 020 7843 6016
www.ncb.org.uk/cpc
Managing Risk in Play: A position statement, *Best Play* and a number of other very useful documents are available to download from the CPC's website.

Details of the Children's Play Information Service can be found at www.ncb.org.uk/library/cpis

PlayBoard
59–65 York Street
Belfast
BT15 1AA
Tel: 028 9080 3380
www.playboard.org

Play Scotland
Midlothian Innovation Centre
Roslin
Midlothian
EH25 9RE
Tel: 0131 440 9070
www.playscotland.org

Play Wales
Baltic House
Mount Stuart Square
Cardiff
CF10 5FH
Tel: 029 2048 6050
www.playwales.org.uk
The First Claim: a framework for quality assessment is available from Play Wales.

The International Play Association – promoting the child's right to play (IPA) www.ipaworld.org provides links to national branches around the world including:

Argentina	www.ipaargentina.org.ar
Canada	www.ipacanada.org
England, Wales and Northern Ireland	www.ipa-ewni.org.uk
Germany	www.ipa-germany.de
Japan	www.ipa-japan.org
Scotland	www.ipascotland.org.uk
Sweden	www.ipa-sweden.org
USA	www.ipausa.org

Australia – there are a number of organisations which would be useful starting points including:

Playgrounds and Recreation Association of Victoria	www.prav.asn.au
Network of Community Activities	www.netoosh.org.au
National Out of School Hours Services Association	www.noshsa.org.au/

Canadian Parks and Recreation Association	www.cpra.ca
This site also contains information from the Canadian Playground Safety Institute (look under 'Training and Education').	

Hong Kong: Playright Children's Play Association	www.playright.org.hk

The Netherlands: Netwerk Ruimte voor de jeugd	www.ruimtevoordejeugd.nl/index.asp

The Republic of Ireland: Sugradh	www.playireland.ie

A selection of interesting and inspiring websites (in alphabetical but no other particular order)

AKiB
AKiB is a federation of adventure playgrounds and children's farms in Berlin. It also lobbies for play space for children and young people in the new German capital. Founded in October 1994 as a result of ten years of work, it is a federation representing its members, but also a medium for qualification and information for children and adults involved in the playwork scene.
www.akib.de/english/english.html

The American Community Gardening Association (ACGA)
ACGA is a bi-national nonprofit membership organisation of professionals, volunteers and supporters of community greening in urban and rural communities.
www.communitygarden.org/

Arvind Gupta
Arvind Gupta's fabulous website is a treasure trove of books and easy-to-make, low cost toys with an educational slant.
www.arvindguptatoys.com/

The Association for the Study of Play (TASP)
TASP promotes research in the study of play and disseminates information through publications and conferences.
www.csuchico.edu/kine/tasp/

The Association of Play Industries (UK)
The trade body within the UK play sector, representing the interests of the manufacturers, installers, designers and distributors of both outdoor and indoor play equipment and safer surfacing.
www.api-play.org/

Child Friendly Cities
A Child Friendly City is a local system of governance committed to fulfilling children's rights.
www.childfriendlycities.org/

Children's Environments Research Group
This group provides an important link between university scholarship and the development of design, policy and programmes that both improve the quality of environments for children and enhance children's interaction with them. It is a branch of the Center for Human Environments, City University of New York.
www.cerg1.org

Children's Landscape, Norway
This website focuses on the interests of children and youth in planning processes. The site provides ideas for modifying school playgrounds, institutions and neighbourhoods in urban areas in order that they cater for the needs of children and young people. Great pictures!
http://home.c2i.net/swan/

The European Federation of City Farms
City Farms are environmental and agriculture projects where children, young people and adults can learn daily about urban and rural environments, their inter-relationship with plants and animals, the importance of the seasons and the relationship between these.
http://efcf.vgc.be/

The European Volunteer Centre
CEV is a European umbrella association of 43 national and regional volunteer centres, that together work to support and promote voluntary activity. It aims to influence policy, strengthen the infrastructure for volunteering in the countries of Europe, promote volunteering and makc it more effective.
www.cev.be/

Foundation for Child Development
FCD is a Thai, non-governmental organisation that aims to support child development in all its forms – body, mind and spirit. Working at an international and grassroots level, the foundation focuses on seeking – and applying – positive solutions to the challenges facing children and youth. Look under 'Family and Community' for play projects.
www.iamchild.org

The Free Play Network
FPN is a network of individuals and organisations which aims to promote the need for better play opportunities for children.
www.freeplaynetwork.org.uk

Growing Up in Cities
GUiC is a global effort to address issues affecting urban children and youth. The initiative enlists the energy and ideas of young people to evaluate their own circumstances, define priorities and create change, and works with them to create better communities. GUiC

has core sites in Australia, Argentina, England, India, Norway, Poland, South Africa and the USA that serve as information centres for their regions.
www.unesco.org/most/guic/guicmain.htm

Guth Airson Iarrtasan Nis (GAIN)

Created from wasteland on the Scottish island of Lewis, this park was designed to blend in with the magnificent landscape. High quality timber equipment was used to create a safe, environmentally friendly play and leisure facility that offers something for everyone.
www.gainplayground.co.uk

Kinetic-Art.Org

This website has contacts for kinetic artists around the world and images which might inspire you to use kinetic art and sculpture as part of the play space.
www.kinetic-art.org/about.asp

London Play

Quality in Play is a quality assurance scheme for out-of-school play and childcare provision and is available from London Play.
www.londonplay.org.uk

Museumnetwork.com

Anyone in the reach of the internet can visit museums and other cultural institutions throughout the world. They can take a virtual tour, make a purchase in the museum shop, and then effortlessly move on to the next museum or gallery they are interested in.
www.museumnetwork.com

The National Playing Fields Association

The core work of The National Playing Fields Association (NPFA) is in protecting and improving playing fields in the UK. Play, sport and informal recreation environments are the focus of the NPFA's action.
www.npfa.co.uk

The Natural Learning Initiative

The purpose of the Natural Learning Initiative is to promote the importance of the natural environment in the daily experience of all children, through environmental design, action research, education, and dissemination of information.
www.naturalearning.org

Play Day

Interesting information about UK national Play Day – billed as a good day out for children but also a way to advocate for children's right to play.
www.playday.org.uk

Play Stories
This site allows playworkers to read and add authentic stories about their work. Be inspired!
www.theinternationale.net/playstories/

Recess please
This website explores important issues about elementary school recess.
www.geocities.com/recessplease/

Sansehaver
Some of Danish landscape architect Helle Nebelong's best known projects in Copenhagen, The Garden of Senses in Faelledparken and the Nature Playground in Valbyparken, are displayed on this rewarding site.
www.sansehaver.dk

The Sensory Trust
A national UK charity, the Trust promotes and implements an inclusive approach to design and management of outdoor space; richer connections between people and place; equality of access for all people, regardless of age, disability or background.
www.sensorytrust.org.uk

VolResource
This is a free source of useful information on anything to do with running a voluntary organisation (whether a community group, charity, or other non-profit body).
www.volresource.org.uk

Wild About Play
Wild About Play is a networking project based in the south west of England to support, develop and promote environmental play – opportunities for children to play freely in and around natural outdoor environments (wild spaces).
www.playwork.co.uk/wildaboutplay

World of Toys
A worldwide celebration of children's creativity and culture through the toys they make.
www.worldplay.org/

Play safety and standards

The rumour mill often works over-time when it comes to playground safety regulations. If someone tells you to cut down a tree or to cover the site in 'safety surfacing' to make a playground meet a notional standard, don't just accept it. Sometimes we need to really advocate for children's play rights! Go back to the actual source of standards for play equipment/environments to ensure that what you are doing is acceptable and then marshal your arguments about the benefits of play to children and the harm done to their development if they are deprived of play.

Regulations vary around the world so the following list is provided as a starting point.

Australia
Australian Playground Safety Institute playground safety courses (in association with RoSPA, see below)
www.eng.uts.edu.au/
ProspectiveStudents/short/
Playgroundsafety.htm

Relevant play equipment standards can be accessed easily by typing play equipment into the search 'enjoy' (some also apply to New Zealand) at: www.standards.org.au/

Canada
Canadian Standards Association
www.csa.ca/
See also Canadian Parks and Recreation Association above.

South Korea
Korean Association for Safer Communities
www.safia.org

UK
The Child Accident Prevention Trust
www.capt.org.uk
Health and Safety Executive
www.hse.gov.uk
Play Safety Forum
www.ncb.org.uk/cpc
RoSPA Play Safety
Tel: 01367 820 988/9
www.rospa.org.uk/playsafety
(has links for Australia, Estonia and Bulgaria)

USA
The National Program for Playground Safety
This site has a number of standards ready to download from the US Consumer Product Safety Commission, the Americans with Disabilities Act (ADA) and the Accessibility Guidelines (ADAAG) for Play Areas.
www.uni.edu/playground
CPSC – info@cpsc.gov) www.cpsc.gov/

Useful contacts – rights

Americans with Disabilities Act
www.usdoj.gov/crt/ada

The Australian Human Rights and Equality Commission has pages for Disability Rights and information on the Disability Discrimination Act 1992.
www.hreoc.gov.au/disability%5Frights/

The Canadian Human Rights Commission
www.chrc-ccdp.ca

Disability Rights Commission (UK) has a range of excellent information and guidance related to the Disability Discrimination Act available in a range of formats.
Tel: 08457 622 633
Textphone: 08457 622 644
www.drc-gb.org

International Save the Children Alliance
www.savethechildren.net/alliance

United Nations Children's Fund (UNICEF)
UNICEF is the branch of the United Nations that focuses on children and youth issues around the world. *The United Nations Convention on the Rights of the Child* can be downloaded from UNICEF.
www.unicef.org/crc

The environment and environmental issues

Centre for Accessible Environments
CAE is a leading authority on the practicalities of inclusion by design, with a mission to share knowledge and expertise through information, training and consultancy.
www.cae.org.uk

European database on environmental toolkits
Access to the largest European database on 'environmental toolkits' – sets of tools (a guide, game, quiz, tips) which aim to change people's behaviour to become more environmentally-friendly.
http://ec.europa.eu/environment/toolkits/index_en.htm

Forest Education Initiative (FEI)
FEI aims to increase the understanding and appreciation, particularly among young people, of the environmental, social, and economic potential of trees, woodlands and forests, and of the link between the tree and everyday wood products.
www.foresteducation.org

Forest Stewardship Council FSC
The FSC accredits independent third party organisations who can certify forest managers and forest product producers to FSC standards. Its product label allows consumers world-wide to recognise products that support the growth of responsible forest management.
www.fsc.org

'Green' directories and information points
www.greenwarehouse.co.uk/
www.guidemegreen.com/
www.recyclenow.com/

GreenSpace
GreenSpace is a registered charity set up to help those committed to the planning, design, management and use of public parks and open spaces.
www.green-space.org.uk/

Grounds for Learning (Scotland)
Grounds for Learning is the schools grounds charity for Scotland, helping schools and early years settings use and develop their grounds to promote positive play, learning and growth.
www.gflscotland.org.uk

Groundwork UK
Groundwork's vision is of a society made up of sustainable communities which are vibrant, healthy and safe, that respect the local and global environment and allow individuals and enterprise to prosper.
www.groundwork.org.uk

Learning through Landscapes
The National School Grounds Charity in the UK, LtL believes that learning and playing outside are essential to every child's development and that improving outdoor spaces in education and childcare can make a real difference. Members can download lots of information including useful information on funding.
www.ltl.org.uk

National Wildlife Federation
Discover how to turn your backyard into a haven for wildlife.
www.nwf.org/backyard/

Plant for Life
Download a free booklet about child-friendly gardening.
www.plantforlife.info/naturesnurture

The World Wildlife Fund
The WWF conserves endangered species, protects threatened habitats and addresses global threats, and aims for long-term solutions that benefit both people and nature.
www.wwf.org.uk

Landscape architecture
The Landscape Institute (UK) is a reference service available to anyone and the online catalogue is for all to search. All queries will be acknowledged and response is usually same day.
www.landscapeinstitute.org/library_and_information_services/

Links can be found at:
www.landscapeinstitute.org/about/past_present_future/links/

American Association of Landscape Architects	www.asla.org/
Australian Institute of Landscape Architecture	www.aila.org.au/
European Foundation for Landscape Architecture	www.efla.org/
Irish Landscape Institute	www.irishlandscapeinstitute.com
International Federation of Landscape Architects	www.ifla.net/
IFLA world	www.iflaonline.org/
World wide members (for example the Hungarian Institute of Landscape Architects)	www.iflaonline.org/members/country/index.html
Society of Garden Designers	www.sgd.org.uk/
Royal Town Planning Institute	www.rtpi.org.uk

Advice on funding

Putting together funding proposals (for trust, individual or corporate donors and so on) need not be too complicated. Potential funders usually require information about the nature of your project, who will benefit and how. Often this will include:

- the rationale – the reason this project is necessary and how you know this;

- aims – what you are hoping to achieve;

- objectives – what you need to do in order to achieve your aims;

- inputs – what needs to be put in (resources, equipment, money, training) to make this happen;

- outputs – what will actually happen;

- outcomes – what the result of all this will be or how things will be different at the end;

- monitoring and evaluation – how you will keep track of progress and how you will find out whether the project has been successful or not in achieving its aims and objectives;

- finances – the project's overall financial situation, what you are asking from the funder, and who else is contributing.

Try to be concise and to the point.

Your application may stand out amongst others if it is clear that the children and the community have been involved in putting plans together. Show that your plans are real by indicating what steps have already been taken (for example, any partner organisations committed to being involved, your own attempts at fundraising, site plans) and what you have been able to achieve so far (through, for example, involving volunteers and community members).

The application can be brought to life with:

- images of the site as it is currently and drawings of how you expect it to turn out;

- quotes and plans in the children's own words;

- quotes from children, parents or staff about what difference the development will make to their lives.

Remember, most potential supporters and funders have their own priorities which you should find out about in advance. Only make an application if you can show that what you want to do will meet their criteria. There are sometimes additional criteria relating to the location or the circumstances of potential beneficiaries of support.

Do think creatively though. The case for funding a play environment (or part of its development) could be put under many headings such as environment, children's learning and development, youth issues, health and wellbeing, physical activity, community safety, inclusion, arts, culture or combinations of these. You do not need to skew your plans, but just set out the case for how the development of a play environment will fit with what the potential funder is interested in supporting.

Bibliography

Alderson, P. and Morrow, U. (2004) *Ethics, Social Research and Consulting with Children and Young People*. Ilford: Barnardo's.

Armitage, M. (2001) The ins and outs of the school playground: children's use of 'play places'. In J.C. Bishop and M. Curtis (eds), *Play Today in the Primary School Playground*. Philadelphia: Open University Press.

Ball, D. J. (2002) *Playgrounds – Risks, Benefits and Choices*. London: Health and Safety Executive.

Bartlett, S., Hart, R., Satterthwaite, D., de la Barra, X. and Missair, A. (1999) *Cities for Children*. London: Earthscan/UNICEF.

Bilton, H. (2002) *Outdoor Play in the Early Years – Management and Innovation*. London: David Fulton.

Bishop, J. C. and Curtis, M. (eds) (2001) *Play Today in the Primary School Playground*. Philadelphia: Open University Press.

Blatchford, P. and Sharp, S. (eds) (1994) *Breaktime and the School: Understanding and Changing Playground Behaviour*. London: Routledge.

Casey, T. (2004) *Play Inclusive (P.inc) Research Report*. Edinburgh: The Yard.

Casey, T. (2005) *Inclusive Play: Practical strategies for working with children aged 3–8*. London: Paul Chapman Publishing.

Casey, T., Manneterm, L. and Chuntawhitate, B. (2001) *Play for Life*. Bangkok: The Foundation for Child Development.

Chawla, L. (2001) 'Putting young old ideas into action: the relevance of growing up in cities to local Agenda 21', *Local Environment*, 6(1): 13–25.

Children in Scotland (2006) *Making Space: Award winning designs for children*. Edinburgh: Children in Scotland.

Children's Play Council (2002) *Making the Case for Play: Building policies and strategies for school-aged children (Children's Play Council Briefing)*. London: National Children's Bureau.

Children's Play Council (2006) *Play Naturally: Survey of children's views*. London: Children's Play Council.

Clark, A and Moss, B. (2005) *Spaces to Play: More Listening to young children using the Mosaic approach*. London: National Children's Bureau.

Claydon, P. (2003) A vernacular of play. In N. Norman (ed.), *An Architecture of Play: a survey of London's adventure playgrounds*. London: Four Corner Books. pp. 27–32.

Department of Culture, Media and Sport (DCMS) (2004) *Getting Serious about Play: A review of children's play*. London: DCMS.

Department for Education (DFE) (1990) *Building Bulletin 71: The outdoor classroom*. London: HMSO.

Department for Education and Employment (DfEE) (2001) *Promoting Play in Out-of-school Childcare*. London: DfEE.

Dunn, K. and Moore, M. (2005) 'Developing accessible play space in the UK: a social model approach', in *Children, Youth and Environments*, 15(1): 331–53.

Ginsberg, O. (2006) 'The farm as a playground', *PlayRights*, January: 8–10.

Groves, M. and Mason, C. (1993) 'The relationship between preference and environment in the school playground'. *Children's Environments*, 10(1): pp 52–9.

Hart, R. (1997) *Children's Participation*. London: Earthscan/UNICEF.

Hendricks, B. (2001) *Designing for Play (Design and the Built Environment)*. London: Ashgate.

Heseltine, P. and Holborn, J. (1987) *Playgrounds: The planning, design and construction of play environments*. London: Mitchell.

Hughes, B. (1996) *Play Environments: A Question of Quality*. London: Playlink.

Hughes, B. (2001) *Evolutionary Playwork and Reflective Analytic Practice*. London: Routledge.

Hughes, B. (2002) *A Playworker's Taxonomy of Play Types* (2nd edn). London: PLAYLINK.

Itoh, T. (1988 [1973]) *Space and Illusion in the Japanese Garden*. New York and Tokyo: John Weatherhill.

Kenny, K. (1996) *Grounds for Learning – A celebration of school site developments in Scotland*. Winchester: Learning through Landscapes.

Lefaivre, L. (2002) Space, place and play. In L. Lefaivre, and I. de Roode (eds), *Aldo van Eyck: the playgrounds and the city*. Rotterdam: NAi Publishers and Stedelijk Museum.

Lefaivre, L. and de Roode, I. (eds) (2002) *Aldo van Eyck: The playgrounds and the city*. Rotterdam: NAi Publishers and Stedelijk Museum.

Lester, S. and Maudsley, M. (2006) *Play, Naturally: A review of children's natural play*. London: Children's Play Council. (Available at www.playday.org.uk)

Mackett, R. (2004) *Making Children's Lives More Active*. London: University College London.

Matthews, H. and Limb, M. (2002) Exploring the 'fourth environment': young people's use of place and views on their environment. *Children 5–16 Research Briefing* No 9. The Economic and Social Research Council. (Available at: www.hull.ac.uk/children5to16 programme/details)

McIntyre, S. (2006a) *Play Inclusive Network 1 Report*. Edinburgh: The Yard.

McIntyre, S. (2006b) *Play Inclusive Network 2 Report*. Edinburgh: The Yard.

Melville, S. (2004) *Places for Play*. London: PlayLink.

Murray, P. (2002) *Disabled Teenagers' Experiences of Access to Inclusive Leisure*. York: Joseph Rowntree Foundation. (Available at: www.jrf.org.uk)

National Playing Fields Association (NPFA) (2000) *Best Play: What play provision should do for children*. London: National Playing Fields Association.

Nicholson, S. (1971) *The Theory of Loose Parts. Landscape Architecture Quarterly*, 62(1) October.

Office of the Deputy Prime Minister (2004) *Developing Accessible Play Space: A Good Practice Guide*. London: Office of the Deputy Prime Minister.

Opie, I. and Opie, P. (1969) *Children's Games in the Street and Playground*. Oxford: Oxford University Press.

Pellegrini, A. D. and Blatchford, P. (2000) *The Child at School: Interactions with peers and teachers*. New York: Oxford University Press.

PlayLink (1999) *Play at School.* London: PlayLink.

Rees, A. (1992) *Building on History*, Scotland Yard Adventure Centre (unpublished paper) Edinburgh.

Sutton-Smith, B. (1997) *The Ambiguity of Play.* Massachusetts: Harvard University Press.

Thomas, G. and Thompson, G. (2004) *A Child's Place*. London: Green Alliance/DEMOS.

Titman, W. (1994) *Special Places, Special People: The hidden curriculum of school grounds*. Godalming: World Wide Fund for Nature/Learning through Landscapes.

UNICEF (1989) *Convention on the Rights of the Child*. (Available at www.unicef.org/crc)

Zini, M. (2006) *Furnishings as a Tool for Education*. In *Senses of Place: Designing Scotland's future schools*. Glasgow: The Lighthouse.

Index

Added to a page number 'f' denotes a figures.

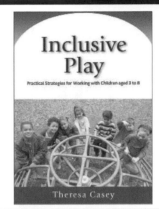

FORTHCOMING...
FROM PAUL CHAPMAN PUBLISHING

Creative Activities for the Early Years

Stella Skinner

Packed full of exciting ideas and powerful visual aids, this book will help those working with young children to encourage and nurture their creativity and imagination. The book takes examples of what has worked in an early years setting, and transfers these inspirational activities onto the page.

The book includes:

- practical activities in art, dance and music and ideas on how to link them together
- advice on how to make the most of music, lighting, space and nursery resources
- showing how the work supports the Foundation Stage curriculum
- ideas for cross-curricular work
- suggestions for recording children's progress
- advice on how to choose materials, and a list of specialist suppliers.

Perfectly suited to nursery practitioners, early years teachers, Sure Start workers, play workers and Children's Centre staff, specialist staff in hospitals and everyone working with young children.

Contents:
Approach to Creative Learning in Early Years \ Visual Arts \ Music \ Dance \ Combined Arts \ Curriculum Guidance \ Materials and Suppliers \ Further Reading

Order on Approval!
We understand how important it is for you to review materials for your school. By ordering your books on approval you have **30 days** to decide whether they suit your needs. If not, simply return in mint condition for a full refund. To order email **education@sagepub.co.uk** (you must provide your school address when ordering).

February 2007 • 120 pages
Paperback (978-1-4129-3448-0) / Hardback (978-1-4129-3447-3)

Paul Chapman Publishing
A SAGE Publications Company

www.PaulChapmanPublishing.co.uk

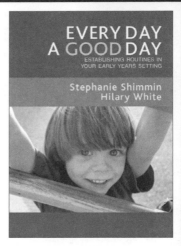